An architectural guide

•••

Peter Howard and Helena Webster
Photographs by Keith Collie

Oxford

An architectural guide

● ● ● ellipsis

•••

BRITISH LIBRARY CATALOGUING IN PUBLICATION
A CIP record for this book is available from the British Library

Oxford: an architectural guide

PUBLISHED BY
Ellipsis London Limited
2 Rufus Street London N1 6PE
E MAIL ...@ellipsis.co.uk
WWW http://www.ellipsis.com
SERIES EDITOR Tom Neville
SERIES DESIGN Jonathan Moberly
AUTHORS PHOTOGRAPH Boyd and
Evans

COPYRIGHT © 1999 Ellipsis London
Limited

PRINTING AND BINDING Hong Kong

ISBN 1 899858 47 4

Helena Webster and Peter Howard 1998

Contents

Introduction

The relationship between Oxford and the university, or 'town and gown' as they are known colloquially, has been one of reciprocal development, and often of tension, since the beginnings of the university in the early Middle Ages. The town's origins derive from Saxon times, when it was a walled enclosure with a grid layout, probably planned. The approximately square shape of that enclosure, centred on Carfax, is still discernible in the present-day street plan. Oxford's importance was as a settlement on a north–south trade route, protected to the south, east and west by marshes and rivers – it is named after a ford through one of the rivers. After the unification of England, when Oxford ceased to be a part of the defensive system against the Danes, it became England's third largest town, after London and Winchester.

By the time of the Norman conquest, when the castle was built, the walls had been extended to the east from Catte Street to the present Longwall Street. The twelfth-century town, dominated by its walls and gates, consisted of houses huddled together in parishes, each with its church. Surrounding the town were several important outlying religious houses, of which Christ Church cathedral, then the church of St Frideswide's priory, is a surviving reminder. Portions of the town walls, rebuilt in 1226–40, also survive.

By the early twelfth century the town had become a centre of learning. The university's focus became the church of St Mary, where the first Congregation House was later added in the early fourteenth century. Students were at first accommodated in hostels, known as academic halls, rented for the purpose, while the teachers, or graduates, lived in colleges. The present-day collegiate system, in which students at the university first have to be members of a college consisting of a permanent body of fellows, started in 1379 when William of Wykeham founded New College for teachers and students alike.

The fourteenth century saw the contraction of the town, which allowed newly founded colleges to build up land holdings within the town walls. New College, for example, acquired a large and notoriously derelict site in the town's north-east corner. The inward-looking quadrangular form of the colleges, which for privacy and defence turned their backs on the often chaotic world outside, was well suited to the orthogonal nature of the town's street pattern. Entered through a gate tower in which the head of the college had his lodgings, the quadrangle's most prominent building was the chapel, an essential setting for the ecclesiastical rites of the college, whose fellows were all in holy orders. Of almost equal importance was the hall, symbol of community, followed by the library and kitchen. Fellows' and students' rooms, accessed in groups by staircases, were ranged cloister-like around the remaining sides of the quadrangle. Beyond, gardens provided for the relaxation of the college members. With the construction of the Divinity School starting in about 1420, the university set a precedent for free-standing buildings within the town.

The design of college buildings in the Middle Ages was in the hands of master masons, including some of the foremost of the time, working under the direction of the benefactor or the agent. The meticulous preservation of college records, often in purpose-built muniment rooms, means that the names of these medieval builders are known, together with the other craftsmen who assisted them. The benefactors, who often gave their names to the colleges they endowed, frequently ensured that they were built to the highest standards, to impress and to last. By contrast with the medley of half-timbered and often improvised buildings of the town, colleges were usually constructed of stone, in an architectural style that compared with the finest buildings of the time. The building of New

College established the practice of placing chapel and hall end-to-end, which was to dominate college design for four centuries.

In the late Middle Ages the academic halls became increasingly redundant and were subsumed into newly formed colleges, while other colleges took over the sites of the now weakened religious houses. Magdalen, for example, was built starting in 1474 on the site of the Hospital of St John east of the town walls, and Cardinal College (now Christ Church) was started in 1525 on the site of the priory of St Frideswide. The large windows and vertical tracery of the Perpendicular period of gothic architecture became widespread, and some buildings, such as St Mary's, the university church, were rebuilt in this style. Beside some fine hammer-beam roofs, the late fifteenth century also saw the construction of two magnificent stone vaults by the master mason William Orchard, in the Divinity School and over the chancel of the priory church of St Frideswide (now the cathedral).

In some ways the development of college building in Oxford mirrors the passage of architectural styles in the country as a whole. However, in sixteenth- and seventeenth-century Oxford, with the exception of such small essays as the gates to the Botanic Garden and the south porch of St Mary's, there is no sudden awakening to the Renaissance. Despite a period of economic revival for both town and university, the designers of college buildings seemed content to perpetuate the established quad-rangular plan, while placing the hall and chapel opposite the entrance, regularising their elevational treatment and introducing a central feature, or frontispiece, to add focus to the composition. Wadham, Oriel and University Colleges, all from the first half of the seventeenth century, are good examples and illustrate well the carefree way in which Renaissance motifs were introduced. The increased density required by a burgeoning university was catered for by building to three storeys, as at Merton Fellows' Quadrangle (1608–10) and the Schools Quadrangle (1613–24), by converting attics of existing buildings to form 'cocklofts', or by building in two storeys with a third attic storey concealed behind repeating small gables, as at Oriel and University Colleges.

Oriel and University Colleges are frequently cited as examples of the innate conservatism of Oxford architecture: both continued building in a virtually unchanged architectural style for over a century. Conservatism, and the high value given to a continuing tradition, is again expressed by Oxford's love affair with the gothic style. Traditionally constructed stone gothic fan-vaults, for example, were in almost continuous use until 1720, when the last one was built in the gateway to Radcliffe Quadrangle at University College. Even Sir Christopher Wren and Nicholas Hawksmoor felt at times constrained to work in the gothic manner. Both produced their own highly individual interpretations of the style, Wren in completing Tom Tower at Christ Church in 1681–82, and Hawksmoor in his 1716–36 rebuilding at All Souls College.

It is to Wren, and his Sheldonian Theatre of 1663–69, that Oxford owes the introduction of classical architecture. Hawksmoor developed the tradition with the Clarendon Building (1711–15), and given his way would have rebuilt the centres of both city and university to a grand classical master-plan. James Gibbs, with the Radcliffe Camera (1737–49), deftly gave the tradition a more overtly baroque face. But it was two academics – Henry Aldrich, Dean of Christ Church, and later Dr George Clarke, Fellow of All Souls – who did most to promote classical design through the early years of the eighteenth century. Both were able designers in their own right, as witness Aldrich's All Saints Church of 1706–08 (now Lincoln College library) and Peckwater Quadrangle (1705–14) for Christ

Church, and Clarke's work at The Queen's College and his library for Christ Church, started in 1717. Their support for Wren and Hawksmoor's architecture, their own design expertise and their ability to work through the master masons John Townesend and his son William, ensured their widespread influence.

Classical Oxford is largely to be found behind the gates of the colleges. Unlike Bath and Cheltenham, the city underwent no major rebuilding in the eighteenth century. Although by then it had for some time been recognised as a beautiful place, improvements were of a small scale and privately initiated. These improvements included building a number of elegant stone houses each side of St Giles' Street, and refacing in stucco and fitting sash windows to many of the remaining late medieval houses, widely surviving today in places such as Holywell Street and Merton Street. The work of the Paving Commission, founded by Act of Parliament in 1771, continued the process of improving the city in the public domain, but it was not until 1826 that Oxford's only new planned classical streets, Beaumont and St John, were developed.

The late eighteenth and early nineteenth centuries saw little new building in the university, and with the exception of James Wyatt, none of the major architects of the period are represented. The Victorian era is another matter. As the nineteenth century passed, growing student numbers, broadening academic interests, increasing affluence, and the dilapidation of many of the older college buildings led to a plethora of restoration and rebuilding. Wyatt and Henry Keene had earlier been involved in reviving the gothic style, but under the influence of the High-Church Oxford Movement this now took on a new seriousness. This sometimes resulted in turgidly misleading evocations of Oxford's medieval past. At its best, however, such as at the University Museum (1855–

60), Keble College (1868–82), and at some of the new parish churches built to serve the expanding suburbs, it produced a carefully considered reworking of the style, based on study of medieval precedents and cogently argued theory.

The twentieth century has seen increased industrial expansion of the city, spurred on by the founding of the Morris Motor Works at Cowley. This has resulted in the growth of large peripheral suburban developments, and the increased commercialisation of the city centre, including, for example, major redevelopments in Cornmarket Street, the construction of ungainly new shopping centres with their attendant multi-storey car parks, and an inner relief road to the west of the historic centre. If much of this is an architectural disaster, it has been matched since the growth of tourism in the 1970s by an increased awareness of the need for conservation. Here, the university and colleges have played a significant role by annexing many of the old houses in the city centre, and through a comprehensive conservation programme carried out under the aegis of the Oxford Historic Buildings Fund.

As ever, the university and the colleges have been responsible for the best and most enduring new building in Oxford, particularly in the post-war period when modern architecture supplanted the early twentieth-century revivalist work of architects such as Basil Champneys, Herbert Baker, Edwin Lutyens and Giles Gilbert Scott. This period has seen the construction of two entirely new colleges by distinguished modern architects, St Catherine's (Arne Jacobsen 1960–64) and Wolfson (Powell and Moya 1969–74). Powell and Moya, Sir Leslie Martin, Arup Associates, Ahrends Burton and Koralek, and more recently MacCormac Jamieson and Prichard, have all been responsible for a number of new buildings, while there have also been notable individual contributions by James Stir-

Oxford: an architectural guide

ling, and Alison and Peter Smithson. While these have all worked in a variety of modern idioms, Raymond Erith at Lady Margaret Hall and Demetri Porphyrios at Magdalen have chosen to work in styles of the past. More recently, some colleges have opted for 'vernacular' schemes, the product of design-and-build, while Keble and St Catherine's have demonstrated that the patronage of modern design is alive and well by employing Rick Mather and Hodder Associates respectively.

FURTHER READING

Colvin, Howard, M, *A Biographical Dictionary of British Architects, 1600–1840*, 3rd edition, Yale University Press, New Haven and London 1995

Colvin, Howard, M, *Unbuilt Oxford*, Yale University Press, New Haven and London 1983

Hinchcliffe, Tanis, *North Oxford*, Yale University Press, New Haven and London 1992

Jebb, M, *The Colleges of Oxford: A Constable Guide*, Constable, London 1992

'Oxford, art and architecture', *Apollo*, CXLV, no. 423, 1997 (a special issue devoted to the city)

Royal Commission on Historical Monuments – An Inventory of the Historical Monuments in the City of Oxford, HMSO, London 1939

Sherwood, J and Pevsner, N, *The Buildings of England: Oxfordshire*, 2nd edition, Penguin, Harmondsworth 1974

Victoria History of the County of Oxfordshire: volumes III, *University of Oxford*; and IV, *City of Oxford*, Oxford University Press, London 1954 and 1979

These works were used as primary source material in the preparation of this book, and we would like to register our gratitude to their authors. We apologise for inaccuracies that may, inadvertently, have crept into our text, and would be happy to be notified of any.

HW and PH

The book's organisation has been made as simple as possible. Buildings are divided into sections relating to typology: the city (covering secular buildings), churches, the university, and colleges. Colleges are then divided into three sections according to location: those to the north-west of St Mary's (the university's church), those to its north-east, and those to its south. Buildings described in each section are ordered chronologically, except in the case of colleges, where the order is alphabetical by college and then chronological under each college.

Below are some pointers to help you find your way around the Oxford colleges:

1. The university has three eight-week terms, running from mid-October to early December, mid-January to mid-March and late April to mid-June. Colleges may have different opening times during term and vacation periods.

2. Colleges are a law unto themselves. They can change opening times or close to visitors at will. Usually it is better to visit colleges in the afternoon.

3. In general, colleges open their grounds, chapel and sometimes hall to visitors. There are private areas, which colleges expect to be treated as such. However, it may well be worth asking at the porter's lodge by the main gateway if you would like to see something not usually open to the public.

4. Always be polite to porters – they can be extremely helpful, or alternatively can make life very difficult!

Many buildings are within walking distance of each other. However, you will probably need a street map for guidance. The best places to obtain one are the Tourist Information Centre, Gloucester Green, or one of the bookshops in Broad Street.

Researching and writing this book has been an adventure and a great pleasure. We hope you enjoy Oxford and its architecture as much as we have.

Helena Webster and Peter Howard

September 1997

The City

Castle

Oxford Castle was built in 1071, six years after the Norman conquest, by Robert D'Oilly, the new Norman governor of Oxford. D'Oilly's mound and enclosing bailey were placed against the western side of the walled Saxon town, necessitating the resiting of the West Gate. After Charles I's failure to hold Oxford, the Parliamentarians in 1651 demolished the bailey wall (rebuilt in the thirteenth century but ruinous by then) and the thirteenth-century stone keep. The mound still survives in part, together with its thirteenth-century well. However, when New Road was constructed under the provisions of the 1771 Improvements Act, it sliced through the mound and destroyed much of the moat.

On the west side of the castle stands St George's Tower. It has four storeys and once belonged to the curtain wall of the bailey, as its thick walls and receding form suggest, but it was appropriated as a bell tower when the castle chapel of St George was founded in 1074. A 1794 recreation of the chapel crypt, which reused the original columns and crudely carved Norman capitals, survives underground behind the tower.

The castle had always been the site of a prison. The present prison buildings (recently closed) were built in 1848–56 to designs by Henry J Underwood, preserving the wings of an earlier scheme of 1785–1805 by George Moneypenny. County Hall stands within the former bailey on the site of the city's earlier Sessions House. Built in 1841 by John Plowman, its thin, battlemented 'Norman' style makes passing reference to the original castle.

ADDRESS Castle mound, Prison and County Hall: New Road; St George's Tower: opposite Paradise Street
ACCESS none; Castle mound and St George's Tower visible from adjacent roads

1071–74 and nineteenth century

1071–74 and nineteenth century

26 and 28 Cornmarket Street

These buildings are the remains of New Inn built by John Gibbs, an Oxford vintner, in 1386. In its original form the inn consisted of a courtyard, running parallel with Cornmarket Street and entered from Ship Street, with domestic ranges to the north and south, and a row five shops facing Cornmarket Street. The north, Ship Street, range was a long building with a stone outer wall and an internal wall of timber framing. The long upper room was probably the main dormitory of the inn, and it was joined to the south range by a small first-floor gallery running above the shops, parallel with Cornmarket Street. The south wing, demolished early this century, may have contained the hall and kitchen of the inn.

Of the original fourteenth-century inn, only three of the five shops and a fragment of the courtyard survive. The shop on the corner of Ship Street and Cornmarket Street is half-timbered, with jettying at the first- and second-floor levels. It was rescued from dereliction in 1950 under the direction of the Oxford architect Thomas Rayson, but, sadly, was over-restored. The six-light window on the upper floor and the heavily carved barge boards have no authenticity.

The other shops are also of three storeys and are half-timbered with an unusual timber gallery running at first-floor level. These were restored in 1987 in a simpler style closer to the original. The ground floor shop fronts are new. A fragment of the courtyard has been incorporated into No. 28 and gives a flavour of the original inn.

ADDRESS 26 and 28 Cornmarket Street
ACCESS No. 28: Monday–Friday 09.30–17.30, Saturday 09.00–18.00, Sunday 11.00–17.00

The City

1386

Golden Cross (formerly Cross Inn)

Golden Cross is an excellent example of a medieval inn built around a courtyard. There was first an inn on the site in the twelfth century, when the landowners, Oseney Abbey, granted a vintner named Mauger permission to convert an existing house to an inn. In 1370 the inn was bought by William of Wykeham for the endowment of New College (pages 234 and 236), and from then became known as Cross Inn.

What is seen today is much rebuilt, yet it retains a picturesque medieval character. The buildings are set around a long, narrow courtyard entered through a gateway from Cornmarket Street. Of the three ranges surrounding the courtyard, the north range (formerly Cross Inn) dates from the fifteenth century and is a two-storey, timber-framed structure finished in stucco, with projecting oriel windows at the first floor, and heavy, coved eaves. The ground-floor shopfronts are modern. In 1927 fragments of simple black and white and more sophisticated coloured Elizabethan wall paintings of grapes and flowers within interlaced, reticulated units were found on the first floor. These can be viewed in the restaurant. The south range (built as Bull, or Summer's, Inn) dates from the seventeenth century and is a three-storey timber-framed structure finished in stucco, with a façade of four gables of three different sizes, and fine double-height oriel windows. The east range, facing Cornmarket, is nineteenth century.

In 1986–87 the whole complex was restored and converted to shops, a restaurant and a new access to the Covered Market (page 36).

ADDRESS 5 Cornmarket Street
ACCESS courtyard open; restaurant open daily 11.00–midnight

Fifteenth century

The City

Fifteenth century

Houses, Holywell Street

The houses in Holywell Street are mostly seventeenth century, but they have received modifications in later years. Many of the original houses are timber-framed, but they were refaced in stucco in the eighteenth century. Nevertheless, the streetscape retains a picturesque medieval character. The houses are now mostly residential accommodation for Wadham College. Of particular note are Nos 3, 13, 35 and 100.

No. 3 is a large seventeenth-century house. For a domestic building, its street frontage is extremely long, with four rooms in a row and a chimney-stack between each pair of rooms. The roof is crossed by four gables. The street elevation has an original two-storey bay, and an arched entry with a fine Georgian hood.

No. 13 has a two-storey rubble façade with a pair of distinctive stone dormers. The windows on the upper floors are the original sixteenth-century versions, but those on the ground floor are eighteenth century.

No. 35 has two storeys and an attic. Its plan is characteristic of an early seventeenth-century house, having a central chimney-stack with stairs at the rear, and a flanking room on each floor. The lower storey is of stone, and predates the timber upper part. The eaves project boldly and are supported by elaborately carved and pierced grotesque brackets, and by large oriel windows. The ground floor windows are eighteenth century.

No. 100 is seventeenth century and has a bold stone gable facing the street. The hollow moulded string courses and window mullions, although eighteenth century, are almost gothic in section. The roof retains its original stone tiles.

The City

ADDRESS 3, 13, 35 and 100 Holywell Street
ACCESS none; visible from Holywell Street

Sixteenth, seventeenth and eighteenth centuries

Sixteenth, seventeenth and eighteenth centuries

The Old Palace

Sitting at right angles to St Aldate's with its main façade facing Rose Place is a timber-framed building now known as The Old Palace. What is seen is largely seventeenth century, built by Thomas Smith, a member of an Oxford family of brewers. However, the lower west part incorporates portions of an earlier sixteenth-century house built by Edward Barkesdale, a tanner, and sold to the Smiths in 1621. The building took its present name in the early nineteenth century, and this was derived from an earlier house on the same site that was reputedly occupied by Robert King, the last Abbot of Oseney and first Bishop of Oxford.

The Rose Place façade consists of a five-gabled east section and a lower two-gabled west section, both with a decorated timber string course at second-floor level, a heavy projecting timber cornice, and two levels of bracketed oriel windows beneath the gables. Each oriel rests on three corbels carved with monsters or other figures merging into scrolls. The elevation is finished with a pargeted design of squares and quadrants, but the design is not original. The shop front facing Rose Place is a twentieth-century addition.

The St Aldate's façade was refronted in 1955 by the architect Russell Cox. It is ashlar-faced with mullioned windows, an embattled parapet and a big, eccentric, curvilinear gable.

The interior still retains some fine sixteenth- and seventeenth-century plastered ceilings on the first floor, and fragments of seventeenth-century timber wall panelling.

The City

ADDRESS 96 and 97 St Aldate's
ACCESS none; visible from St Aldate's and Rose Place

Sixteenth, seventeenth and twentieth centuries

Sixteenth, seventeenth and twentieth centuries

Stone's Almshouses

Stone's Almshouses were founded in 1700 by the executors of the Reverend William Stone, Principal of New Inn Hall (now St Peter's College), as a charitable provision for the poor of the parish of St Clement's. The building was designed and built by Bartholomew Peisley II, a member of one of Oxford's most celebrated families of master masons and quarry-owners. The accommodation consists of eight tenements, four on each floor, symmetrically located about an open passage which gives access to the rear of the building from St Clement's Street. The upper tenements are reached via two staircases at the rear. Above the passageway is a meeting room.

The symmetrical façade of the two-storey stone building is restrained and dignified, and sits back from the street behind a low stone wall. The elevation is composed of eleven bays. The pedimented middle bay, which contains the arched passage, projects slightly and has a crossed window at first-floor level. The pediment is decorated with a cartouche-of-arms and also a scrolled cartouche containing the inscription: 'This Hospital for ye poor and sick was founded by the Reverend Mr. William Stone, Principal of New Inne Hall, In hopes of thy assistance Ao. Dni. 1700.' There is a communal garden to the rear.

The almshouses are now owned and managed by the trustees of the City of Oxford Charities.

ADDRESS 247 St Clement's Street
ACCESS none; visible from St Clement's Street

Bartholomew Peisley II (master mason) 1700

Bartholomew Peisley II (master mason) 1700

St Giles' House

This imposing stone house, arguably the best of its period in Oxford, was built for MP Thomas Rowney in 1702. From 1852 the house served as the Judge's Lodging, and from 1875 to 1878 as Oxford High School for Girls. It is now owned by St John's College. The design is tentatively attributed to the Oxford master mason Bartholomew Peisley II.

The house sits back behind a stone wall, which has grand piers surmounted by urns. The two-storey, ashlar-faced, symmetrical street elevation is an early example of classicism in Oxford (although it is not clear how much is due to the eighteenth-century remodelling). The three central projecting bays are capped by a pediment, while the cornice, string courses and quoins give the elevation strength and elegance. In the centre, the main entrance is raised four steps above the forecourt, and is given further emphasis by a stone door-case with pilasters and a straight entablature. The door-case is probably eighteenth-century, and replaced the original, more distinguished, shell hood. The dropped first-floor cills and the four-gabled dormer windows were also part of the eighteenth-century remodelling, but the attic dormers may have replaced originals. The interior has original plaster ceilings, a staircase with twisted balusters, and seventeenth-century bolection-moulded panelling.

In the garden is a building in the classical style. Its domed roof was a working scale model for the stone dome originally proposed by James Gibbs for the Radcliffe Camera (page 112) before it was decided to use a timber dome instead.

ADDRESS 16 St Giles' Street
ACCESS none; visible from St Giles' Street

Bartholomew Peisley II (master mason) 1702

Bartholomew Peisley II (master mason) 1702

Vanbrugh House

The original house on the site was probably built in the seventeenth century, but was refaced in 1721. The design of the imposing façade is often attributed to Sir John Vanbrugh, but is more likely to have been by Bartholomew Peisley III in the manner of Vanbrugh. Peisley was from a notable Oxford family of master masons and quarry-owners: he had previously worked with Vanbrugh at Blenheim Palace, and also collaborated with William Townesend on the building of the steeple of All Saints Church, High Street, in 1718–20. Peisley probably refaced the house for his own use, as it is recorded that he died there in 1727.

The façade is a good Vanbrughian imitation. The three-storey composition is built in ashlar, and consists of five bays, the central bay projecting slightly. The round-headed central doorway with its big triple keystone is flanked by heavy Doric pilasters that rise through two storeys to straddle the first-floor window, and are capped by a deeply projecting cornice supported on just two brackets in the form of triglyphs. On the second floor the pilasters run through to the projecting cornice at roof level. To each side of the central bay the detailing is more restrained. The ground-floor windows are plain, while those at first-floor level have squared aprons and keystones. The second-floor windows have segmental heads and keystones. The bold, baroque modulation of the façade can be compared with Nicholas Hawksmoor's Clarendon Building (page 110), finished only seven years earlier. The interior still retains some eighteenth-century wall panelling and the original eighteenth-century staircase.

ADDRESS 20 St Michael's Street
ACCESS none; visible from St Michael's Street

The City

Bartholomew Peisley III (master mason) 1721

Bartholomew Peisley III (master mason) 1721

Radcliffe Infirmary

The Radcliffe Infirmary was the first Oxford county hospital, and was made possible by funds given by the trustees of the will of John Radcliffe, the successful London physician. It was intended to house 68 patients in four wards. The buildings were designed by Stiff Leadbetter, Surveyor to St Paul's Cathedral (1756–66) and architect of Gloucester County Hospital (1758–61), but were completed by John Sanderson of London following Leadbetter's death in 1766. Leadbetter had the reputation of designing in a competent, but dull, Palladian manner, and the Radcliffe Infirmary was no exception.

The original infirmary building faces Woodstock Road, forming the west range of an entrance forecourt. It is in a classical manner with 13 bays and three storeys, and is an ashlar range with the end and three central bays slightly projecting: the central bays are given further emphasis by a pediment. The door, door-case and window of the entrance are twentieth century. Inside there is a fine central staircase leading to a first-floor balcony, which looks over the entrance hall. On the ground floor there is an interesting vaulted corridor that originally gave access to the wards.

Over the years the hospital has expanded in an unplanned, piecemeal way. The only other building of interest is the chapel, which forms the north range of the entrance forecourt. It was built in 1864 to a design by Sir Arthur Blomfield.

The terracotta triton fountain in the centre of the forecourt was designed by John Bell in 1857.

ADDRESS Woodstock Road, south end
ACCESS all enquiries telephone 01865 311188

Stiff Leadbetter and John Sanderson 1759–70

The City

Stiff Leadbetter and John Sanderson 1759–70

Covered Market

The Covered Market was built in 1773–4 by the Paving Commissioners as part of a general attempt to tidy up the congested and insanitary public areas of the city. The street markets, including the Butter Bench in Carfax, Butcher Row in Queen Street, and Fish Lane in St Aldate's, were rehoused in new premises. The designer of the new Covered Market was John Gwynn of Shrewsbury, Surveyor to the Commissioners of the Oxford Paving Act, who also designed Magdalen Bridge in 1772–90.

Over the years the market has been modified greatly, but the plan form remains, and parts of the original buildings still exist. The market stretches from High Street, through the centre of the block, to Market Street (formerly Jesus Lane). The range to High Street, known as Oxford Parade or New Parade, is original and has a classical pedimented façade of ashlar. Each of the three entrances to the market aisles is marked by a pedimented window. The market buildings that lie behind this range comprise blocks of stalls, with storage accommodation above, separated by arcades running north–south and east–west. The original blocks had open walkways between them, but in the 1880s–90s the stalls were progressively rebuilt and the walkways covered with a timber roof forming double-height arcades with clerestory windows, giving a light and airy atmosphere. The painted timber stalls and roof to the arcades are particularly charming, especially at the wide east end of the east–west arcade. At the Market Street end the market is bounded by the original high wall which is pierced by three gates.

The market still sells produce to the colleges, as it did in the eighteenth century.

ADDRESS Market Street, Cornmarket Street and High Street
ACCESS Monday–Saturday 08.00–17.00

John Gwynn 1773–4

John Gwynn 1773–4

Beaumont Street and St John Street

Beaumont and St John Streets were the first of the St John's College speculative developments in north Oxford. The impetus for building Beaumont Street was the desire of Worcester College to forge a road link with the city. The scheme was conceived in 1736, but difficulties in reclaiming the leases on the land meant that development did not start until the 1820s.

In 1822 Henry Dixon, a surveyor, laid out the land for an 18-metre-wide road and residential building plots, and the architect William Garbett was commissioned to draw up designs, which consisted of terraces of Georgian houses, designed as a unified composition, in a style reminiscent of the late Georgian developments in Bath. The resulting development was less consistent than intended because of the difficulties in ensuring that the numerous lessees built strictly to Garbett's design. In the event, the development was not completed until the early 1840s, the first years of the Victorian age, by which time its Georgian style looked dated. Nevertheless Beaumont Street, which was intended to appeal to the social pretensions of professionals and members of the university, is particularly fine with its restrained ashlar façades, unarticulated window openings, applied cast-iron balconies and classical door-cases.

St John Street runs north from Beaumont Street, on axis with the Radcliffe Observatory (page 152), though this view is now partly obscured by later development. The terraces are more modest in scale and detail, and were intended to appeal to a more humble clientele.

ADDRESS Beaumont Street and St John Street
ACCESS none; fronts visible from Beaumont Street and St John Street; rear of St John Street visible from Beaumont Buildings

The City

William Garbett 1828–40s

William Garbett 1828–40s

Martyrs' Memorial

The Martyrs' Memorial occupies a commanding position at the south end of St Giles' Street, Oxford's widest street. The martyrs commemorated are Bishops Latimer and Ridley and Archbishop Cranmer, burnt alive at the stake in 1555–56 during the reign of the catholic Queen Mary for refusing to recant their protestant beliefs. They died nearby, a spot now marked in Broad Street, in a ditch outside the city walls near the prison.

Nearly 300 years later a competition was held to raise a memorial to the bishops, to counterbalance the rising High-Church Oxford Movement. The energetic George Gilbert Scott won with a design based closely on the Eleanor Cross at Waltham. It is not clear why a memorial to a catholic queen who died in 1290 was a fitting model for the martyrs, but the competition appealed to Scott's enthusiasm for A W N Pugin, whose *Contrasts*, extolling the moral virtues of gothic architecture, had appeared in 1836. It also coincided with the foundation in 1839 of the Oxford Society for the Study of Gothic Architecture, and with an increasingly serious archaeological approach to gothic architecture, particularly that of the late thirteenth century.

Like the Eleanor Cross, the Martyrs' Memorial is six sided, a suitable geometry for a trinity of martyrs. It has three stages: the lowest has pointed arches with diaper patterning in the spandrels; in the middle statues stand below pinnacled ogee arches; and at the top is a slender spire, also of three tiers. Interestingly, Charles R Cockerell's classical Ashmolean Museum (page 116) was started the same year on a site across the road, a coincidence that foreshadowed the mid-nineteenth-century 'battle of the styles'.

ADDRESS St Giles' Street, south end
ACCESS open

Sir George Gilbert Scott 1841–43

Isis House

This piece of Victorian gothic whimsy, which Nikolaus Pevsner called 'a bit of a joke', was built in 1848 by Joseph Cauldwell, an eccentric accountant. It is said that Cauldwell built it in the form of a castle to defend himself from marauding undergraduates.

Isis House sits on an island on the city side of Folly Bridge, the existing version of which was built in 1825 by Ebenezer Perry. Folly Bridge used to be called South Bridge, but was renamed in the seventeenth century after the old tower or 'folly' that was the toll-gate at the southern end. South Bridge replaced a succession of earlier bridges that carried Grand-pont, a great causeway of eighth-century origin that formed the southern approach to Oxford over the river Isis. The Thames in Oxford has been known as the Isis – after the Egyptian goddess – since 1535 when the name was first used in the writings of John Leyland. Isis appeared officially in a statute of George II in 1751 and has been used ever since.

The long, narrow, castle-like house has two major elevations, one to St Aldate's, which is tower-like and one bay wide, and the other to the river, which is a long elevation rising dramatically from the water's edge. A stone base faces the river and is surmounted by a simple, rectangular, three-storey block of buff-coloured Oxford stock brick divided into panels by vertical and horizontal bands of red and blue brick dressings. The river façade is a particularly romantic composition with its irregularly sized openings, projecting bay window, decorative iron balconies and canopy, and niches with white plaster sculptures. The elevations are further decorated with brickwork, used as rustication around openings, as quoins and string courses, and as crenellations at parapet level.

ADDRESS St Aldate's
ACCESS none; visible from St Aldate's and river walk

The City

Joseph Cauldwell 1849

Joseph Cauldwell 1849

Park Town

Park Town was the first planned residential development on the outlying land to the north of Oxford. The 3.6-hectare isolated plot ran as a narrow strip eastwards from Banbury Road and was surrounded by land belonging to St John's College. The plot belonged to the Board of Guardians of the Oxford Workhouse and was originally intended for a new workhouse to replace one adjacent to the Radcliffe Infirmary (page 34). The workhouse was eventually built in Cowley, and the guardians instead decided to develop the land for middle-class housing. Both Edward G Bruton and Samuel Lipscomb Seckham submitted designs, but it was Seckham's regency design that was selected.

Seckham's scheme was an ingenious attempt to reconcile the commercial and aesthetic demands of the time. His solution was to design a mixture of terraces and villas. At the east end a raised terrace of relatively small houses closes off the estate. The bulk of the estate, two facing crescents, runs lengthways down opposite sides of the site with a communal garden in the central area. Between the terrace and the central crescents are semi-detached houses and stable blocks of rustic design. At the entrance to Banbury Road there are large, vaguely Italianate, villas standing in their own gardens and forming a loose crescent. Planting on the central island screens the development from Banbury Road.

By 1854 building had begun on the two crescents, and in 1855 they and the terrace at the east end were complete. The remaining lots, intended for detached and semi-detached villas, were taken up more slowly, and two plots were never built on.

ADDRESS Park Town, Woodstock Road
ACCESS none; visible from Park Town Terrace and Park Town Crescent

Samuel Lipscomb Seckham 1853–60

Samuel Lipscomb Seckham 1853–60

Norham Manor Estate

In the mid-nineteenth century St John's College responded to the growing demand for middle-class housing by engaging in the speculative development of their 121-hectare north Oxford estate. The greater part, adjacent to the University Parks and known as Norham Manor Estate, was to be dedicated to detached and semi-detached villas, while the north–south strip to the west of Banbury Road was laid out with terraces and smaller houses for the lower-middle and working classes.

William Wilkinson was commissioned by the college to produce a layout and house designs for the estate to satisfy the middle-class demand for self-contained houses set in large gardens, close to town. The layout consisted of broad, tree-lined streets dividing the land into large urban blocks, which were in turn subdivided into smaller plots suitable for large houses set back from the street in generous gardens. By selling the land as individual leasehold plots of good size, and by requiring all designs to be approved by their architect, St John's controlled the style and quality of the building. Hence the suburb acquired its distinctive and remarkably consistent picturesque brick Venetian gothic character, even though it took over 20 years to complete. The development might be seen as a precursor of the early twentieth-century garden suburb.

The villas on the east side of the Banbury Road (Nos 56, 58, 60 and 62) were built for individual middle-class clients and they formed a gothic showpiece at the entrance to the new suburb. Nos 56 (1866) and 58 (1865–67) were designed by John Gibbs, the builder; No. 60 (1865–66) by William Wilkinson himself; and No. 62 (1864–65) by the local architect Edward G Bruton.

ADDRESS 56, 58, 60 and 62 Banbury Road and Norham Gardens
ACCESS none; visible from Banbury Road

William Wilkinson, John Gibbs and Edward G Bruton 1860–80s

William Wilkinson, John Gibbs and Edward G Bruton 1860–80s

Randolph Hotel

William Wilkinson was a successful local architect who was surveyor of the Norham Manor Estate (page 46), where he also designed many of the houses in a Venetian gothic style. The Randolph Hotel is Norham Manor writ large.

As appropriate for a building of the early years of the railway age, the hotel dominates its corner site, providing a reassuring commercial presence for the increasing number of visitors to the city. It would be hard to imagine a greater contrast with the rest of Beaumont Street, completed less than 30 years earlier in a simple Georgian style. The building is of brick, not stone; the street elevation is heavily modelled with projecting wings and oriel windows; the roofline is energetic. The architectural style comes close to admitting the hotel to the small group of mid-nineteenth-century buildings in Oxford – such as the University Museum (page 118) and Keble College (page 156) – which were influenced by John Ruskin's love of Venetian gothic.

The hotel takes its name from Sir Francis Randolph, an early benefactor of the Ashmolean Museum (page 116), its opposite neighbour. In 1952 the hotel was made even larger by being extended along Beaumont Street in a style matching the existing work.

ADDRESS Beaumont Street, at corner of Magdalen Street.
ACCESS open

William Wilkinson 1864–66

William Wilkinson 1864–66

Christ Church Old Buildings

In the mid-nineteenth century the pace of building in Oxford slackened, yet there were sporadic attempts to redevelop some of the worst housing in the old city. In 1866, slums in the parish of St Thomas, between The Hamel and Woodbine Place, were demolished on the orders of the Dean and Chapter of Christ Church, and replaced by Christ Church Old Buildings, a block of 30 residential flats built as model dwellings. The flats are arranged around a three-sided communal courtyard and are accessed from the street via open staircases. Each self-contained dwelling originally provided a sitting room and three bedrooms, together with a scullery, WC, ashpit, sink and separate water supply – accommodation that was progressive at the time.

The building has a restrained architectural character reminiscent of nineteenth-century tenements in London funded by charitable organisations such as the Guinness Trust and Peabody Trust. The elevation to the street has large, flat façades of red brickwork modulated by horizontal bands of buff Oxford stock brick, small window openings and open staircases. The latter, one on each elevation, have unusual arched heads with keystones flanked by brick roundels. The elevation of the courtyard is also restrained, but has slightly more generous window openings relating to the major rooms in the flats. The window cills and heads, steps and landings demonstrate an innovative use of cement concrete.

In 1893 Christ Church built a second tenement block in Hollybush Row, known as Christ Church New Buildings. These are the only two tenement-type developments in the city.

ADDRESS Woodbine Place
ACCESS none; visible from The Hamel and Woodbine Place

Edward G Bruton 1866–67

Edward G Bruton 1866–67

27 and 29 Banbury Road

'Queen Anne' emerged in the 1850s as a style suited for the new middle classes. Richard Norman Shaw had invented it, based on a revival of the red-brick architecture of seventeenth- and eighteenth-century town houses. He worked almost exclusively in London, and his houses in Cheyne Walk, Chelsea, typify the style. John J Stevenson's two houses in Banbury Road were the first of the few Queen Anne houses in Oxford. No. 29 was built for Stevenson's brother in law, Thomas Omond, bursar of St John's College; No. 27 was for the philosopher Thomas H Green. On the front of No. 27 is a terracotta plaque bearing the initials of Green and his wife.

The plans of the two houses follow the Oxford gothic villa model, an overgrown cottage rather than a reduced mansion; however, the elevations are quintessential Queen Anne. The style is characterised here by the use of prominent roofs and chimney stacks, asymmetrically composed red brick façades with paired or elongated white-painted sash windows, red moulded brick embrasures, applied bay windows and fancy oriels, wooden balconies, and decorative brick panels of sunflowers, swags and cherubs. The use of red brickwork was particularly unusual for Victorian north Oxford. In his book on the period, *Sweetness and Light* (1977), the architectural historian Mark Girouard called the two houses 'unassuming, but never dull, pleasantly irregular but never quaint, ... among the best Queen Anne'.

The houses are now owned by St Anne's College.

ADDRESS 27 and 29 Banbury Road
ACCESS none; visible from Banbury Road and from garden of St Anne's College

John J Stevenson 1880–81

John J Stevenson 1880–81

Town Hall

The 1893 competition to replace the eighteenth-century Palladian town hall was won by Henry T Hare with a showy 'Jacobethan' design that owed much stylistically to Sir Thomas G Jackson's work at the Examination Schools (page 122). Here the same ingredients – Jacobean gables, turrets with ogee roofs, pilasters surmounted by a frieze, and arched mullioned windows, some in the form of oriels – are assembled, though less successfully, into a largely symmetrical façade designed to impress. However, the effect seems altogether too grand and too busy for the streetscape of St Aldate's. The elevation to Blue Boar Street, on the other hand, is much quieter and more enjoyable, and the timber cupola is a good addition to the Oxford skyline.

The interiors continue the heavily ornamented Jacobethan theme in the public spaces – the entrance lobby, staircase, Great Hall and Council Chamber: a case of overwhelming civic opulence.

On the corner of St Aldate's and Blue Boar Street, a small fifteenth-century crypt was incorporated into the town hall. This now forms part of the Museum of Oxford, which engagingly tells the story of the city's development.

Hare also designed the decidedly more successful Midland Bank and Tower House that flank St Martin's tower at Carfax, just north of the town hall.

ADDRESS St Aldate's
ACCESS town hall: limited access during office hours; Museum of Oxford: Tuesday–Saturday 10.00–17.00; admission charge

Henry T Hare 1893–97

The City

Henry T Hare 1893–97

The Old School (now Tourist Information Centre)

The Central Schools came under the Oxford Schools Board in 1898 and several new schools were built to the designs of Leonard Stokes, an already established designer of London schools.

The Old School (formerly Central School for Boys) was built on the site of some old cottages at the northern edge of Gloucester Green market. Stokes designed the building in a fluent, yet informal, Arts and Crafts style. The central portion of the building is of stone in two storeys, and to each side there are single-storey brick wings. The entrance is through a pointed gothic doorway with blind Perpendicular panelling above, flanked by canted bay windows, to one side of which there is a magnificent tall chimney. The plan was ingenious. The cloakrooms and service spaces were located symmetrically about the entrance and were intended to lessen noise from the market. The entrance lobby led directly to a large circular hall with a central cupola. The classrooms were located off this central space, which was meant to be both the functional and symbolic heart of the school.

The building now houses a public house and the Tourist Information Centre. Unfortunately the pub's arts and crafts interior has largely been obliterated.

ADDRESS Gloucester Green
ACCESS Tourist Information Centre: Monday–Saturday 09.00–17.30, Sunday and public holidays in summer 10.30–13.00, 13.30–15.30, telephone 01865 726871; The Old School (public house): Monday–Saturday 11.00–23.00, Sunday 12.00–22.30

Leonard Stokes 1901

Leonard Stokes 1901

Belsyre Court

This building complex was conceived at the tail end of the St John's College speculative development projects on their land in north Oxford; Beaumont Street and St John Street were the first such developments, in the 1820s (page 38). The site was first considered for a theatre but by 1932 a scheme for a mixed development of shops, offices and service flats was decided on. The flats were aimed at retired and single residents who wished to live in the area but found the villas on the Norham Manor Estate too big and expensive (page 46). A first design by J C Leeds was rejected by the college, and they subsequently commissioned Ernest R Barrow, who had previously designed college rooms and flats for Sidney Sussex College, Cambridge.

Barrow's design consists of a five-storey building wrapping around three sides of a pleasant landscaped courtyard, with the open side facing south. Shops, with offices and flats above, front the Woodstock Road, while the other two ranges only contain flats. The architecture is a curious mixture of styles. The overall composition is in a rather dour Jacobean revival style, with brick façades articulated by gabled bays, steeply pitched roofs, and windows with Jacobean mullions. However, there is also a classical colonnade providing covered access to the shops facing a lay-by off the Woodstock Road. The courtyard uses the Jacobean revival style consistently and has pleasant brick bay windows and large balconies with timber balustrades facing south over the garden, but the effect is slightly detracted from by the numerous externally fixed services.

ADDRESS 65 Woodstock Road
ACCESS none; visible from Woodstock Road, Plantation Road and St Bernard's Road

Ernest R Barrow 1936

Ernest R Barrow 1936

Oxford Playhouse

The first Oxford Playhouse opened in 1923 as a home for the Oxford Repertory Company and was located in the Red Barn at the St Giles' Street end of the Woodstock Road. The theatre closed in 1934 due to financial problems, but almost immediately funds were raised by the loyal local audience, and in 1936 Edward Maufe was commissioned to design a new theatre on a vacant site leased from St John's College. Maufe had previously done minor work for St John's and went on to design Dolphin Quadrangle in 1948.

The site was a broad plot within the Georgian terraces on the south side of Beaumont Street. Maufe's design simply completed the street frontage with a three-storey ashlar façade which extended the language of the adjacent Georgian terrace, though in a centralised, rather than incremental, form. The only stylistic difference is the main entrance which hints at art deco with its curved walls, columns, and glitzy canopy of coloured glass and bronze framing. The rear of the building is a functional brick design, which faces a service yard.

Numerous internal refurbishments have occurred over the years, so although the shell remains intact the decorative scheme bears no resemblance to Maufe's original. The front of house is straightforward, with the entrance to the stalls ahead, flanking staircases leading to the circle, and a first floor foyer overlooking Beaumont Street. The auditorium has a traditional proscenium arch layout and is functional but unremarkable.

ADDRESS Beaumont Street
ACCESS interior: apply to Box Office, telephone 01865 798600; visible from Beaumont Street

Sir Edward Maufe 1938

Sir Edward Maufe 1938

Museum of Modern Art (MOMA)

The Museum of Modern Art was founded in 1966 by a group of Oxford art enthusiasts, and was conceived originally as a gallery to house a permanent collection of post-1945 art. Its first premises, with a revised remit for the display of changing exhibitions, were located in King Edward Street. In the early 1960s the City of Oxford purchased the vacant early nineteenth-century Hall's Brewery storehouse in Pembroke Street, and in 1970 leased the front part to MOMA. The original storehouse was built for Hanley's Brewery: it was greatly extended to the rear in 1878 and in 1908 the complex was sold to Hall's, a rival Oxford brewery.

The original modest refurbishment for MOMA was designed by its then chairman Trevor Green, an Oxford architect. Fund raising led to expansion in 1981 with the opening of the Piper Gallery, taking up more of the original storehouse. Further improvements in the 1980s included the remodelling of the Pembroke Street entrance, providing a covered open colonnade giving direct access down to a basement café and up to a new entrance foyer. The architects were the Glaswegian practice Gillespie Kidd and Coia, who had previously designed Blackwell's Music Shop (page 68).

MOMA is particularly interesting as an early example of the reuse of a redundant building. The warehouse's variously sized spaces and their arrangement gives the museum a distinctive character. The two galleries on the upper floor are large, double-height volumes open to the roof and are particularly good for showing large artworks.

ADDRESS 30 Pembroke Street
ACCESS Tuesday–Wednesday and Friday–Saturday 10.00–18.00, Thursday 10.00–21.00, Sunday 14.00–18.00; admission charge

Trevor Green 1964, 1981, Gillespie Kidd and Coia 1986

The City

The City

Trevor Green 1964, 1981, Gillespie Kidd and Coia 1986

John Radcliffe Hospital

Commissioned as a replacement for the Radcliffe Infirmary (page 34), this vast teaching hospital is visible as a series of monumental white blocks on a hillside to the north-east of the city centre at Headington. Yorke Rosenberg and Mardall were appointed by the governors of the United Oxford Hospitals in 1964 to prepare a master plan for the development of the 28-hectare site. The development was planned in three phases, the completed hospital containing 1500 beds, a new medical school with extensive postgraduate research laboratories, and staff residential accommodation.

The YRM strategy divided the accommodation into monofunctional megablocks laid out as geometrically aligned objects set in a hard landscape, with little regard to the topography of the site. The main hospital block is a huge, eight-storey monolith. The ground and first floors form a solid podium and are air conditioned, while the upper floors are planned around four open courtyards and are ventilated naturally. The third level has bay-width slots carved out of the building on each side, allowing views from the courtyards to the external world. The building is clad in white ceramic tiles, a hallmark of YRM buildings of that date.

The design of large hospitals is a difficult task and YRM succeeded in producing a coherent minimal architecture influenced by the work of Ludwig Mies van der Rohe. However, the result is severe and intimidating for the user, and reflects the values of a period when the rational logic of the hospital as mechanism took precedent over the psychological well-being of the user.

ADDRESS Osler Road
ACCESS public areas accessible at most hours; visible from internal access road

The City

Yorke Rosenberg and Mardall 1968–72

The City

Yorke Rosenberg and Mardall 1968–72

Templeton College

Ahrends Burton and Koralek came to prominence in 1961 with a winning design for a new library at Trinity College, Dublin. By 1969 they were working in Oxford at Keble College (page 158) and the Oxford Centre for Management Studies, later renamed Templeton College after a benefactor.

The college occupies a heavily landscaped hilltop in green-belt country to the south of Oxford. The college's brief was for the first blocks of residential accommodation to be capable of a six-fold phased expansion, and for a building whose modern design would be a challenging experience for the more conservative sectors of British management.

The buildings are approached from the car parks up a tree-studded hill past flowing water, and are grouped defensively at the top, somewhat in the manner of a small Italian hill town. Within the complex, walkways float above landscaped courtyards, linking the detached residential wings into the more compact central communal block. The form and materials chosen by ABK were unashamedly modern. On the outer faces of the backward-stepping residential wings a white *in-situ* concrete frame is infilled with zinc-covered panels, while sloping glazed sections cover the south-facing rooms, which look into the courtyards. Fair-faced concrete blockwork is used elsewhere, inside and out.

ADDRESS Kennington Road, Iffley, near Upper Road
ACCESS by appointment

Ahrends Burton and Koralek 1969–90

Ahrends Burton and Koralek 1969–90

Blackwell's Music Shop

In the 1970s Blackwell's Bookshop increased its retail outlets in Oxford by developing with Wadham College a small infill site in Holywell Street for a new music bookshop and additional fellows' rooms. The architects were the Glaswegian practice Gillespie Kidd and Coia, who subsequently refurbished the Museum of Modern Art (page 62).

Although the street façade is narrow, the site is deep. The design puts the bookshop at ground and lower-ground levels on the Holywell Street frontage with fellows' rooms above. To the rear is a tiny, one-storey, open quadrangle, Holywell Court, surrounded by more fellows' rooms and screened from the college by a pre-existing stone wall and a new, first-floor, landscaped courtyard.

Set in the medieval context of Holywell Street, the design deliberately sought a modern frontage that took cues from neighbouring buildings. At the first floor there is a deep string course that ties in with the first-floor level of adjacent buildings. Above and below, the elevation recedes at an angle: above in slate to a clerestory window strip to fellows' rooms, below in stepped concrete to a glazed shopfront and entrance.

Internally, beyond the low entrance, the shop's space opens out by dropping to lower-ground level. The double-height space is surrounded by a gallery at ground-floor level and is flooded with light from a large, centrally placed, inverted glass funnel. Shelving is tucked under the ground-floor gallery and simply lines the perimeter of the space. Solid materials – timber, stone, slate, lead and bronze – are used with minimal detailing to give an air of quality and robustness.

ADDRESS Holywell Street
ACCESS Monday and Wednesday–Saturday 09.00–18.00, Tuesday 09.30–18.00, Sunday 11.00–17.00

The City

Gillespie Kidd and Coia 1971–72

Gillespie Kidd and Coia 1971–72

Thackley End

Thackley End was commissioned by Abacus Housing Association in 1972 and is an early example of housing association flats. Built on a deep site with a frontage to Banbury Road, the scheme consists of a group of four detached four-storey blocks set in communal gardens. The garden side of each block reads as a series of *in-situ* concrete decks infilled with storey-height glazing. The decks are stepped back along the major façade, providing each flat with part of a continuous balcony. The overall impression is slightly reminiscent of a ziggurat.

The entrance side of the blocks, which provides access and parking, is plainer, giving the impression of a functional service yard rather than a decorous entrance court. The expressed concrete frame is simply infilled with fair-faced blockwork, although some modulation is given by the access stair towers, which have curved ends infilled with Profilit glass walls. The internal walls of the flats are also of fair-faced blockwork.

The design is a fluent essay in the late-brutalist aesthetic and has strong stylistic affinities with college work of the same period by better-known architects, such as Powell and Moya's Wolfson College (page 264). True to its age, it has little in common with the Victorian villas surrounding it.

ADDRESS 119 Banbury Road
ACCESS none; visible from Banbury Road and entrance drive

Bernard Hartley and Partners 1972

Bernard Hartley and Partners 1972

Oxford Ice Rink

Oxford is famous for the skating on the iced-over flood plain of Port Meadow in the winter months. In 1980 the Oxford Ice Skating Trust was formed and raised money for a new indoor skating rink. The city council took over the project and commissioned Nicholas Grimshaw and Partners to design a building for Oxpens Recreational Field, an unpromising site in the contextless west side of Oxford by the inner ring road.

The building is an essay in 'High-Tech' architecture. The accommodation sits under a single, large-span roof (72 x 38 metres), the rink taking up the front of the plan, with two storeys of ancillary accommodation behind. The building is entered on the mezzanine level via a long ramp which runs externally along its length.

Two distinctive 30-metre-high masts support a beam which runs the full length of the building and carries most of the roof loading. This structural display was justified by the poor ground conditions. With this solution 80 per cent of the roof loading is taken by the piled foundations of the masts, allowing the external wall columns to bear on shallow pad foundations. The building is given further nautical imagery by using portholes for windows. Yet the overall effect is rather drab, not helped by the grey PVC-coated glass-reinforced concrete wall cladding, the grey singleply PVC membrane roof, and the poorly maintained external landscaping. However, the building is saved by the vast glass wall that forms the elevation to Oxpens Road, allowing views to and from the ice rink which animate the building delightfully, particularly at night.

ADDRESS Oxpens Road
ACCESS daily 10.00–22.30; visible from Oxpens Road; admission charge

Nicholas Grimshaw and Partners 1984

Nicholas Grimshaw and Partners 1984

Gloucester Green

Gloucester Green had been used variously over the centuries as the site for a city gaol, a weekly cattle market (1797–1931) and latterly a car park and bus station. In the late 1980s the city council, which owned the site, finally responded to an age-old local controversy regarding the site's under-utilisation, by inviting designs from six developer/architect teams for a mixed-use development. The winning scheme, designed by Kenrick Associates, proposed a mix of shops, houses, market square, underground public car park and bus station.

The scheme has two linked public squares, the larger for the market, the smaller for the bus station, both of which are bounded by three-storey, mixed-use buildings with attics. The urban spaces are rather clumsily proportioned, and the hard landscape design is uninspired and of poor-quality materials. In addition the bus station square is too small to handle the growing volume of buses and coaches, leaving little room for pedestrians.

One aspect of the scheme that has resulted in much debate is the 'pick-and-mix' architectural style. Attempting to respond to the context, the architects plucked forms, materials and details eclectically from the surroundings, combining them with art nouveau-inspired features to make stylistically confused brick skins for steel-framed structures. Although infinitely preferable to the drab design of the 1970s Westgate Shopping Centre, the architecture is of a disappointing quality considering the status of Oxford as a major heritage city.

The City

ADDRESS Gloucester Street
ACCESS open

Kenrick Associates 1990

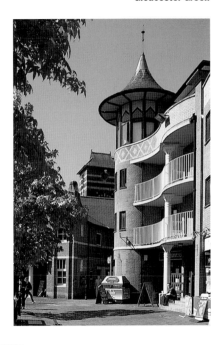

Kenrick Associates 1990

Churches

St Michael at the North Gate

The joy of St Michael is its late Anglo-Saxon tower, which is probably the oldest remaining building in Oxford. The original Saxon church of St Michael at the North Gate stood just inside the north entrance to the city, and was built sometime between 1000 and 1050, not long after the first city walls were constructed. The tower must have been a useful lookout, and a blocked doorway high in its north wall hints at a direct connection with the ramparts of the city wall.

The tower's forthright square silhouette, the 'long and short' corner stone construction, the baluster-shaped columns and deep capitals supporting the stilted round arches of the small openings in the upper two storeys are all characteristic of the Carolingian influence in architecture just before the Norman conquest. Unfortunately nothing remains either of the north gate, which was cleared away in 1771 as part of the city improvements, or of the Saxon church itself. The present church originally dates from the thirteenth century, although the chancel and south chapel are all that remain from that period. The north chapel and transept were added in the next century, while late in the fifteenth century the main body of the church and the north aisle were entirely rebuilt, and a porch rebuilt on the south side.

The church underwent a major restoration by George Edmund Street in 1854, and was again restored after a severe fire in 1953. The steel and glass visitor centre outside the north aisle was designed by John Perryman in 1994. It leads to the tower, which houses a history of the medieval city around the north gate, and from the top of which there is a good view.

ADDRESS Cornmarket Street, by Ship Street
ACCESS tower: Monday–Saturday 10.00–17.00, Sunday 12.30–17.00
(closes winter at 16.00, and during services)

Churches

Eleventh and thirteenth–fifteenth centuries

Churches

Eleventh and thirteenth–fifteenth centuries

St Mary the Virgin, Iffley

The parish church of the village of Iffley, south of Oxford, was built in 1175–82 by Robert de St Remi. It is a well-preserved Norman church with much of its original decoration, and consists of a nave, which in plan is a double square, a square choir located beneath a massive tower, and a chancel. This too was originally square (possibly with an apse), but in the mid-thirteenth century it was doubled in size with the addition of another bay to the east, and remodelled with new windows.

Although simple in form, the church is renowned for its carving. The west doorway is heavily ornamented with beakhead and zigzag decoration, and with signs of the zodiac and symbols of the evangelists; the south doorway, flanked by carved columns with elaborate capitals, is even more lavish. Inside, the tower arches are heavily carved, and flanked by shafts of black 'marble' from Purbeck in Dorset, an early use of this material. The rib vault of the original chancel has zigzag carving and a central boss decorated with dragon's heads.

The church has seen few changes. Late in the fifteenth century some nave windows were replaced, leaving the westernmost ones intact. In 1621 a battlemented parapet was added to the nave. In the nineteenth century the west gable was restored, and a circular window reintroduced above the west doorway.

In the churchyard, a yew tree, reputed to be a thousand years old, overhangs a medieval cross. The adjacent rectory, remodelled in the sixteenth century, conceals a house dating from shortly after the time of the church. The Thames flows gently nearby.

ADDRESS Church Way, Iffley
ACCESS May–September daily 14.00–17.00; October–April, Saturday–Sunday 14.00–17.00 generally, if the weather is fine

Robert de St Remi 1175–82

Robert de St Remi 1175–82

St Cross, Holywell

The manor of Holywell, named after a spring just by the church, lay just outside medieval Oxford. Despite being owned by Merton College, it carefully guarded its independence from the city until 1667. In the Middle Ages St Cross was a chapel of St Peter-in-the-East (page 258). It is now a small, though rather undistinguished, parish church, embodying a comfortable amalgam of successive alterations and rebuildings.

The chancel and chancel arch, the earliest remaining parts, survive from the mid-twelfth century. A tower was added in the thirteenth century, and the aisles extended on each side of it. In the fifteenth century the north arcade was rebuilt and the top stage of the squat tower added, giving the west front a central feature. As part of a nineteenth-century restoration by John M Derick, the north aisle was rebuilt in 1837–38 (though retaining the fifteenth-century arcade), as were the south aisle and arcade in 1843–44.

To the north of the church a few parts of the 1516 rebuilding of Holywell Manor remain, now as part of Balliol College.

ADDRESS St Cross Road, by Manor Road
ACCESS see church noticeboard for availability of key

Twelfth–nineteenth centuries

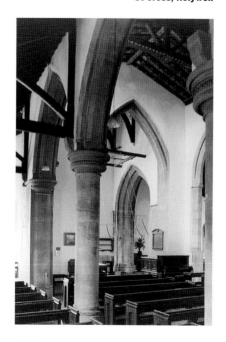

Churches

Twelfth–nineteenth centuries

St Martin's Tower

St Martin's Tower is the remaining bell tower of a church whose nave once projected into Cornmarket Street. The first church on the site dated from the eleventh century, but was demolished in 1820 and rebuilt by Thomas Harris and John Plowman, supposedly to a design inspired by Gloucester Cathedral. It in turn was demolished in 1896 by order of the Paving Commissioners in an attempt to relieve congestion at Carfax. The demolition of the body of the church was part of an extensive redevelopment scheme for Carfax, designed by Sir Thomas G Jackson, which also included the removal of the Butter Bench and the rebuilding of the four corner buildings. The Midland Bank (1896) and Tower House (1896) are by Henry T Hare, who also designed the Town Hall (page 54), Martins Bank (now Abbey National) is by Ashley and Newman (1930–31), and Lloyds Bank is by Stephen Salter with R C Davey (1900–01).

In both nineteenth-century redevelopments the thirteenth-century tower of St Martin's was kept. The castellated rubble stone tower was restored in 1898 by Jackson as part of his redevelopment scheme for Carfax. He added a stair turret and buttresses, and moved the west doorway and the seventeenth-century clock to the east side, effectively turning the tower back to front. The clock was fitted with two-quarter jack-bells, and at the same time the original two quarter-boys were replaced by replicas. (The originals – so called because they strike each quarter hour – are now in the Oxford Museum; page 54.) Below the clock are the city's arms, inscribed with its motto 'fortis est veritas'.

The tower can be climbed and affords good views of central Oxford.

ADDRESS Carfax
ACCESS open daily April–October 10.00–17.30, November–March
10.00–15.00; admission charge

Thirteenth century

Thirteenth century

St Mary the Virgin, University Church

St Mary was originally associated with the east gate of the Saxon town. By the thirteenth century the gate had moved further east, and the growing university had co-opted the church for its own use. It has remained the University Church and is also the parish church of the city.

The tower, from which the views are excellent, was built *c*.1280 and is the oldest part of the present building; the spire, with its exuberant pinnacles decorated with ballflowers, was added *c*.1310–20. The building was given a greater presence in the cityscape by the opening up of the north side with the completion in 1748 of Radcliffe Square (page 112).

Adjoining the east side of the tower is the university's first Congregation House, which was built in 1320–27. A library was started above it at the same time, although it was not completed until 1411. (This was in use until Humphrey, Duke of Gloucester's library (page 98) replaced it in 1489.) The North Chapel, to the west of the tower, was also built around the 1320s. In 1503–10 both were given matching Perpendicular gothic windows, and the library was reroofed, unifying the north elevation of the church. This was shortly after the chancel had been entirely rebuilt in 1463, followed by the nave and aisles in 1490–1503, making the present church almost entirely Perpendicular gothic in style.

The grandly exotic ceremonial south entrance porch of 1637, with its improbable conjunction of Raphaelesque twisted columns, Serlian decoration and fan vault, may have been designed by Nicholas Stone who had recently completed gateways at the Botanic Garden (page 104).

ADDRESS High Street and Radcliffe Square
ACCESS open daily 09.00–17.00 (July and August 09.00–19.00); tower, admission charge

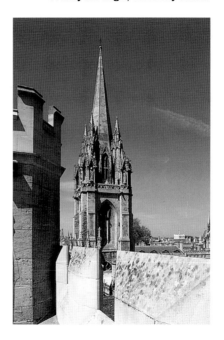

Churches

Thirteenth–seventeenth centuries

St Mary Magdalen

In the twelfth century the parish church of St Mary Magdalen served a busy suburb that had sprung up just outside the walled city, at a point where the roads from Northampton and the Cotswolds joined in the wide area now known as St Giles' Street, before entering the north gate.

The building has grown and changed from the Middle Ages through a process of accretion and successive restorations, and is now wide and spacious. The original parts were the nave, chancel and south aisle, but these were rebuilt in the early sixteenth century in the Perpendicular gothic style, leaving only the thirteenth-century east window. The tower and south porch were added in 1511–31, although the rendered finish and battlements are from an 1872 restoration. The south chapel (originally a lady chapel) and its crypt are the earliest parts of the present building and date from 1320, but the ornate exterior buttresses facing the graveyard are replicas of the originals, and the statues were set in them only in 1914.

The north aisle, known as the Martyrs' Aisle, was added in 1842 to designs by Sir George Gilbert Scott and his partner William B Moffatt, using funds remaining from the public appeal for the Martyrs' Memorial (page 40). This is said to be the earliest attempt in Oxford to recreate an archaeologically correct gothic interior. Scott and Moffatt also carried out a general restoration of the church at the time, ironically doing away with some of the older features in the process.

ADDRESS Magdalen Street
ACCESS open during services: Monday–Saturday 11.00, 18.00; Sunday 08.00, 10.30, 17.30

Churches

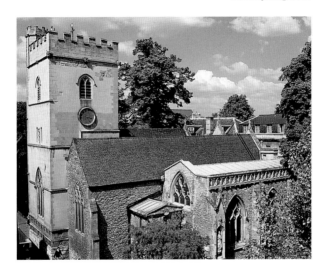

Thirteenth–nineteenth centuries

St Philip and St James

George Edmund Street was a keen ecclesiologist, who at the age of 27 was appointed Oxford Diocesan Architect. From his Oxford office in Beaumont Street, where Philip Webb and William Morris were both at one time assistants, he produced designs for churches and associated buildings in the diocese. These included in 1852–54 the rectory for St Ebbe's in Paradise Square, and in 1853 the theological college at Cuddesdon, just outside the city.

St Philip and St James was commissioned as a parish church for the affluent new residential suburbs of gothic north Oxford (page 46). Despite the 1855 publication of Street's *Brick and Marble in the Middle Ages, Notes of a Tour in the North of Italy*, which influenced his contemporary designs for St James the Less, Westminster, the style of St Philip and St James owes more to English and French thirteenth-century gothic architecture, which were his other great loves.

The general effect is one of massiveness, emphasised by simple features such as lancet windows and flat plate tracery. A substantial tower rises over the chancel, and is surmounted by a stubby broach spire. Roughly finished Bath stone is enhanced by bands of red sandstone, providing the horizontality and constructional polychromy so beloved of the period. Inside, the grandeur of Street's nave arcade is abruptly interrupted by the chancel wall, and the last bay is canted in towards the chancel arch, directing the nave towards the sanctuary. The interior has recently been sensitively adapted for use as the Oxford Centre for Mission Studies.

ADDRESS Woodstock Road, by Church Walk
ACCESS interior: apply to bursar, telephone 01865 56071; visible from Woodstock Road

George Edmund Street 1860–66

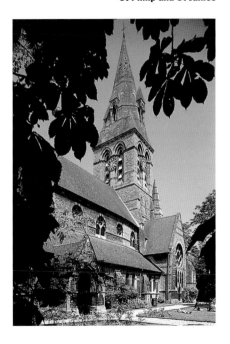

George Edmund Street 1860–66

St Barnabas

The tall Italianate *campanile* of St Barnabas is a prominent landmark in Jericho, the Victorian working-class quarter it was built to serve. The church's benefactor was Thomas Combe, the Anglo-Catholic superintendent of The Clarendon Press (page 114), whose employees lived in the small terraced houses round about St Barnabas.

Sir Arthur W Blomfield, the son of a bishop, was Combe's architect, and he chose to work in the Italian romanesque style – an interesting Anglo-Catholic contrast with the thirteenth-century gothic of Samuel S Teulon's contemporary St Frideswide, Oseney (page 94). Blomfield's church was a simple aisled basilica, with a semicircular apse at the east end and a rose window above an apsidal baptistery at the west end. It is a church that might almost have been built in Ravenna or Rome in the twelfth century. The bell tower was originally free-standing but was joined to the church in 1887. It is stylistically later, having pointed gothic openings in the upper stages which contrast with the round-arched windows below. The aisle windows and porch are more inventive in their rectilinear detailing.

Blomfield, charged by Combe to make a cheap building combining strength and solidity, originally considered using mass concrete, an early proposal for the material. However, rubble and roughcast proved less costly, and this he enlivened with bands of red brick and spidery quoins. In 1888–89 Blomfield added the north aisle, and later decorated the east end. Further decoration has been added to the north wall of the nave, giving the interior a rich, mosaic-like appearance. Heads of Combe and Blomfield have been identified carved on capitals at the west end.

ADDRESS Cardigan Street
ACCESS see church noticeboard for availability of key

Sir Arthur W Blomfield 1869–72

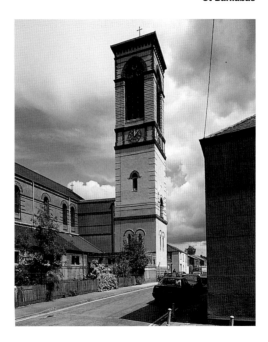

Sir Arthur W Blomfield 1869–72

St Frideswide, Oseney

Frideswide was a Saxon who founded a priory in Oxford, supposedly out of gratitude for her miraculous deliverance from an importunate suitor. The priory was dissolved in 1524 (page 270), but the dedication was revived for this small Victorian church, built to serve the new working-class suburb of Oseney, and designed by the London architect Samuel S Teulon.

Teulon's early work was characterised by his great use of polychromy and his inventive use of gothic motifs, but this church, designed at the end of his life, is altogether plainer and marks the passing of the age when banded stonework was fashionable. Here, a simple aisleless nave of rough stone is terminated by a stumpy octagonal tower over the choir, beyond which is a polygonal apse. The windows are plain paired lancets, with flat plate tracery used at the east and west ends. On the north side is a low transept enclosed by massive tower buttresses which flank a rose window in the tower. Inside, the main tower arches appear to be carried on small columns, in turn supported by conical corbels.

The tower was intended to carry a spire, which had it been as exciting as the tower at Teulon's St Mary, Ealing, of the same period, would have been a thrilling addition. As it is, the unfinished tower and blocky external capitals, which remain uncarved, give this church a squat rudeness. The adjacent vicarage and charming linking passage, designed by Harry G W Drinkwater, are somewhat later.

ADDRESS Botley Road, near West Street
ACCESS open most days 09.00–17.00

Samuel S Teulon 1870–72

Churches

Samuel S Teulon 1870–72

The University

Bodleian Library, Divinity School

Work on the university's new Divinity School started in 1423 under Richard Winchcombe. It was to be a single-storey rectangular building of five bays, with the main doorway at the west end. Lack of resources meant slow progress, and in 1439 a new mason, Thomas Elkyn, simplified the details. A second storey was added five years later for the collection of books that Humphrey, Duke of Gloucester had given to the university.

In 1480, as a result of a gift by Thomas Kemp, Bishop of London, a stone vault was added on the ground floor. The design was probably by William Orchard, who was employed at Magdalen College (page 224), and who may have worked on the vault at Christ Church Cathedral (page 270). Four major cross arches were constructed with pairs of stone, lantern-like, pendant voussoirs, from which elaborate lierne vaults fan out to many carved stone bosses. The building was opened in 1490.

In 1610–12 the Proscholium (page 100), was added across the east gable, providing a new entrance, while in 1634–37 the Seldon End was built, obliterating the original west entrance and its flanking towers, and making the plan H-shaped. The Seldon End houses the Convocation House and Chancellor's Court under mid-eighteenth-century fan vaults, with a galleried extension of the library above. The gothic ogee doorway of 1669 on the north side of the Divinity School is perhaps by Sir Christopher Wren.

ADDRESS Broad Street and Catte Street.
ACCESS interior: Monday–Friday 09.00–17.00, Saturday 09.00–12.30 (children under 14 not admitted); guided tours March–end October: Monday–Friday 10.30, 11.30, 14.00, 15.00, Saturday 10.30, 11.30; admission charge; south side visible from garden of Exeter College

Winchcombe, Elkyn and Orchard (master masons) 1423–90

The University

Winchcombe, Elkyn and Orchard (master masons) 1423–90

Bodleian Library, Proscholium

By the late sixteenth century, Humphrey, Duke of Gloucester's library had been dispersed as a result of the Reformation, and the Divinity School (page 98) was in poor condition. Sir Thomas Bodley, scholar and diplomat under Elizabeth I, whose name is given to the present university library, restored and rearranged the building as a new library from 1598 to 1602. Bodley gave many books and encouraged other's gifts.

The original rectangular building, with the Divinity School on the ground floor, was soon too small, and Bodley proposed that a new wing, known as the Arts End, be built across the east gable, making the building T-shaped. The ground floor forms a new entrance and wide lobby, or Proscholium, to the Divinity School, whose original east doorway is preserved inside. The first-floor library extension is galleried and is the first instance in Oxford of wall bookshelves being used, rather than bookstalls.

Although started 120 years after the Divinity School was completed, the Proscholium conservatively uses the same design motifs. The string courses and narrow blind panels in the Perpendicular gothic style that adorned the original east gable of the Divinity School (and are still visible on the side buttresses) were copied on the elevations, and the original Perpendicular gothic gable window was recreated above a new classical doorway. This in turn was given a gothic ogee head. The stone vault built inside the ground floor relates well to that used in the Divinity School built some 130 years previously.

The University

ADDRESS Broad Street and Catte Street
ACCESS Monday–Friday 09.00–17.00, Saturday 09.00–12.30

John Akroyd (master mason) 1610–12

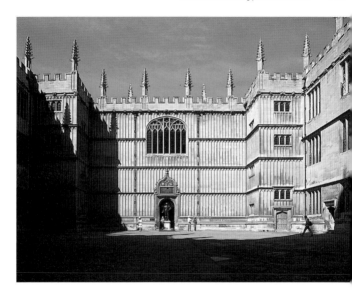

John Akroyd (master mason) 1610–12

Bodleian Library, Schools Quadrangle

After his death in 1613 Sir Thomas Bodley's will provided for a substantial expansion of the library he had founded, as soon as an adjacent site became available. Construction was overseen by Sir Henry Savile, cofounder of the library and warden of Merton College, where he had recently finished building the Fellows' Quadrangle (page 296). The expansion is a similar three-storey quadrangle built on the front of Bodley's Proscholium (page 100), which had been completed the previous year. The lower two floors were for the University Schools, with the library on the top floor. Staircase towers occupy the internal corners, two extending the Proscholium in the same style. The main entrance to the quadrangle is from Catte Street, through a gate tower on axis with the Proscholium, with lesser entrances in the centre of the adjacent ranges.

The masons were all from Yorkshire, and they produced a fine, though conventional, building of stark functionality. Rectangular gothic cusped windows are arranged uniformly on stone façades modulated by string courses, rainwater pipes and pinnacles.

Facing the Proscholium, on the inner face of the gate tower, is a magnificent ceremonial frontispiece of five superimposed classical orders. This piece of applied grandeur, heavily decorated with grotesques and strapwork, derives from the influence of Italian, French and Lowland pattern books such as those published by Sebastiano Serlio. The canopied statue is of James I flanked by Fame and University. However, by that time Inigo Jones was already introducing a purer and more refined form of classicism, and the tower, however enthusiastic, belongs to an earlier generation.

ADDRESS Catte Street
ACCESS Monday–Saturday 09.00–17.00, Sunday 09.00–12.30

John Akroyd, John and Michael Bentley (master masons) 1613–24

The University

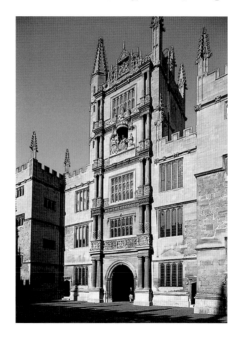

The University

John Akroyd, John and Michael Bentley (master masons) 1613–24

Botanic Garden, Main Gateway

Oxford's Physic Garden was founded in 1621, the first in Britain. Ten years later Nicholas Stone was engaged to build three gateways in the walls of the rectangular plot, all of which survive. He had worked with Inigo Jones on the Banqueting House in Whitehall, London, was a leading monumental sculptor, and in 1632 was appointed Master Mason to Charles I.

Compared with Jones' cool Palladianism, the main gateway is a fantastical affair of superimposed pediments and mannerist bands of alternating smooth and rusticated stonework. The design, modelled on the pattern of a Roman triumphal arch, draws heavily on a volume of monumental gateways published in France in 1551 by the Italian Sebastiano Serlio, and widely used in northern Europe as a pattern book. The main, and two lesser gateways make a delightful ensemble in the Italian manner.

The University

ADDRESS High Street, opposite Magdalen College
ACCESS garden open daily 09.00–17.00 (winter 09.00–16.30); main gateway visible from High Street

Nicholas Stone 1632–33

Nicholas Stone 1632–33

Sheldonian Theatre

The Sheldonian Theatre was commissioned by the university as a place of ceremony and assembly, having been made possible by Gilbert Sheldon, Archbishop of Canterbury. The designer was Sir Christopher Wren, then Savilian Professor of Astronomy at Oxford.

This was the first building in Oxford in the classical style, though not the first in England. Wren chose the ancient Roman theatre as his model, making the building D-shaped in plan.

Inside, the building has no stage, and the focus of attention is the Vice-Chancellor's chair facing the steeply tiered seating, which follows the curve of the building. Wren again departed from the Roman model by incorporating a 21-metre timber-trussed roof, which won acclaim from contemporaries. The roof structure supports a ceiling painted in the manner of an open sky above a canvas awning, by Robert Streeter.

On the exterior, the ceremonial entrance faces the Divinity School (page 98) across a courtyard, and has a central pediment reminiscent of Andrea Palladio's churches. The remaining D-shaped elevation is treated as two stages: a rusticated blind-arcaded lower part, with a pilastered clerestory above. The north doorway facing Broad Street has a richly carved surround of garlands, a cornice on corbels, and a central trophy above. Wren's boundary to Broad Street has railings and stone plinths surmounted by huge stone bearded heads in the form of herms, or guardians of a sacred site. They were renewed in 1868 and 1972. The octagonal cupola was added by Edward Blore in 1838 as a replacement for Wren's smaller original.

ADDRESS Broad Street
ACCESS Monday–Saturday 10.00–12.45, 14.00–16.45 (November–February closes at 15.45); admission charge

Sir Christopher Wren 1664–69

Sir Christopher Wren 1664–69

108

The Museum of the History of Science (formerly The Old Ashmolean)

The commissioning of a new building to house the collection of natural curiosities given to the university by Elias Ashmole in 1677 acknowledged the natural sciences as a subject suitable for academic endeavour. The museum was built on part of the town ditch, with the line of the city wall marking the rear boundary of the site.

The building's design, attributed to the master mason Thomas Wood, is indebted stylistically to Sir Christopher Wren's Sheldonian Theatre (see page 106), but lacks its innovative qualities. The main rooms are on two floors with a half basement, in a simple, rectangular block of five bays. The east elevation, facing the theatre, is dominated by a grand ceremonial doorway with pairs of Corinthian columns supporting a segmental pediment. The fine carving is attributed to William Bird. The elevation to Broad Street has five bays of close-set cross windows with alternating triangular and segmental pediments, and a square-headed entrance doorway placed centrally.

The internal plan has a rectangular room on each floor. The basement, once used as the chemical laboratory, is lit from an area between the building and the railings fronting Broad Street. The colonnade of Ionic columns along the length of the ground-floor room is nineteenth century. A rear extension housing a heavy well-type staircase allows access to the upper floor. The staircase to the basement was added in 1833.

The building became The Museum of The History of Science in 1924 when the original collections were dispersed to other university institutions.

ADDRESS Broad Street, adjacent to the Sheldonian Theatre
ACCESS Monday–Friday 10.30–13.00, 14.30–16.00

Thomas Wood (master mason) 1679–83

The Clarendon Building

The Clarendon Building (now the University Registry) was built to rehouse the university presses from the basement of the Sheldonian Theatre, and was later named after the 1st Earl of Clarendon, whose profits from his *History of the Rebellion* led to its funding. The building needed to house the Bible and the Learned Books presses, and Nicholas Hawksmoor, in competition with John James and William Townesend, produced five designs all showing the presses united by a central passage. This effectively acts as a triumphal arch leading from Broad Street to the Bodleian Library Schools Quadrangle (page 102) beyond. Hawksmoor received the commission while working with Sir John Vanbrugh on Blenheim Palace, and he was introduced to the university by Dr George Clarke, Fellow of All Souls, himself an architect and patron, whose collection of architectural drawings is preserved at Worcester College. This was Hawksmoor's first commission in Oxford, and he later designed for All Souls and The Queen's College (pages 208 and 246).

As built, the four-square building is a key compositional element at the heart of the university, and it formed part of Hawksmoor's unrealised master-plan for the city centre. The Doric portico, which projects into Broad Street, is gravely classical and austere in its verticality, and is accentuated by a high basement. Deeply recessed windows under shallow arches, chunky keystones in a complex rhythm of wall planes, a pronounced entablature and the projecting cornice all contribute to the heavy modelling and baroque grandeur of Hawksmoor's mature work. On the roof are lead muses by James Thornhill, and there is a fine iron entrance gate, all contemporary with the building.

ADDRESS Broad Street
ACCESS none; visible from Broad Street

Nicholas Hawksmoor 1712–15

The University

The University

Nicholas Hawksmoor 1712–15

Radcliffe Camera

Dr John Radcliffe, a London physician, wished to be immortalised by commissioning a library for the university's science collections. Early designs by Nicholas Hawksmoor for a building attached to the Bodleian Library were abandoned on Radcliffe's death in 1715. At this point the trustees of Radcliffe's will appointed James Gibbs to assist Hawksmoor in producing a fresh design resited in the newly formed Radcliffe Square. On Hawksmoor's death in 1736 Gibbs was entrusted with the building's completion. Despite his desire totally to redesign the building, the trustees only allowed Gibbs to make stylistic alterations to the original design.

Hawksmoor's design took the external form of a mausoleum, being circular in plan with an open colonnade at ground-floor level (now enclosed) and a domed roof. Gibbs, who had been taught by Carlo Fontana in Rome, transformed Hawksmoor's essentially classical conception into a sophisticated piece of Italian mannerism. A heavily modelled, rusticated ground floor forms the base for the main drum, which is divided into alternate wide and narrow bays by paired Corinthian three-quarter columns. The drum supports a deep entablature, stone balustrades and urns, in the manner of a peristyle. Above the drum sits a smaller circular drum and the dome.

The interior is more restrained and owes something to domed churches of the Italian Baroque. There is a high, domed reading room on the first floor surrounded by an ambulatory and gallery housing the books. Eight piers and arches carry the drum and coffered dome. The plasterwork is by Giuseppe Artari and Giovanni Bagutti.

ADDRESS Radcliffe Square
ACCESS none; visible from Radcliffe Square

Nicholas Hawksmoor 1712–36 and James Gibbs 1715–48

The University

The University

Nicholas Hawksmoor 1712–36 and James Gibbs 1715–48

Oxford University Press

In the early nineteenth century the Clarendon Press, now known as Oxford University Press, had outgrown the Clarendon Building (page 110). A green-field site on the edge of Oxford was found for a new printing house. The layout for the new buildings rejected the obvious factory model, preferring the collegiate model with its four ranges planned around a quadrangle. Inside the large quadrangle the Bible press occupied the south wing and the Learned press the north wing. The Walton Street entrance front and the south range were designed by Daniel Robertson, while the north and west ranges are attributed to Edward Blore. Both architects had a reputation for designing stone buildings in a consistent but rather stolid classical style, and the Press buildings were no exception.

The Walton Street frontage consists of projecting wings with end pavilions to each side of an entrance block. The façades of the wings are divided into bays by pilasters, each bay containing square-headed windows with brackets and hoods. In the centre is a monumental entrance modelled on an ancient triumphal arch. It has a deep attic and entablature supported on four giant Corinthian columns. The end pavilions are of a matching scale but more simply modelled. They are three bays wide and two storeys high, with an attic storey in the entablature. The façades have angled pilasters and two central giant Corinthian columns matching the entrance block. The elevational treatment inside the quadrangle is plain.

The Press has expanded over the years but unfortunately none of the later buildings are of any architectural note.

ADDRESS 35 Walton Street
ACCESS none; visible from Walton Street

Daniel Robertson 1826–28, Edward Blore 1829–30

The University

Daniel Robertson 1826–28, Edward Blore 1829–30

Ashmolean Museum and Taylorian Institute

In the early nineteenth century the university decided to bring together its collections of art and antiquity, including that of Elias Ashmole, and to provide new accommodation for the Taylorian Institute. A prominent site was purchased from Worcester College on the corner of Beaumont Street (page 38) and St Giles' Street, and Sir Charles R Cockerell was entrusted with the design. Cockerell responded with a building in a monumental neo-classical style inspired by the Temple of Apollo at Bassae, which marked his stylistic transition from strict Grecian to a freer, more baroque manner. The plan is H-shaped with two monumental pavilions joined by a long, windowless lower block facing Beaumont Street. The elevation of the joining block is subdivided into bays by giant pilasters and has a centrally placed tetrastyle portico marking the main entrance. The flanking pavilion to St Giles' Street houses the Taylorian Institute; the mirroring pavilion houses galleries. They are built of buff Bath stone with applied pilasters of white Portland stone to subdivide the elevation into bays. Detached fluted Ionic columns, deep friezes, and entablatures contribute to their monumentality. The sculpture in the tympanum of the entrance pediment and the figures on the St Giles' Street front, depicting France, Italy, Germany and Spain, are by W G Nicholl.

Recent alterations in 1996, including a café, shop and lecture theatre under the courtyard, were designed by Stanton Williams Architects in a minimalist style.

ADDRESS Beaumont Street, opposite Randolph Hotel
ACCESS Tuesday–Saturday 10.00–16.00, Sunday 14.00–16.00, Bank Holiday Monday 14.00–17.00; closed Good Friday and Easter Monday, and during St Giles' Fair in early September

Charles Robert Cockerell 1841–45

The University

Charles Robert Cockerell 1841–45

University Museum

When, somewhat belatedly in 1849, the university founded a school of natural sciences, an architectural competition for a new building was held. The project's leading proponent was Henry Acland, who was a friend of John Ruskin, the art critic and champion of gothic architecture.

Not surprisingly, the winning scheme by Benjamin Woodward of the Dublin practice Deane, Son and Woodward was not a classical design, but one influenced by Ruskin's enthusiasm for Venetian gothic. Across the main block Woodward put freely spaced Venetian windows on string courses, while his steep roof and central entrance tower are possibly more reminiscent of northern gothic town halls. Behind, lecture halls and demonstration rooms were organised more informally around a quadrangle housing an encyclopaedic display of the world's natural sciences, while to one side the chemistry laboratory was a witty evocation of the abbot's thirteenth-century kitchen at Glastonbury Abbey.

Inside, the two-storey cloister surrounds a gently top-lit hall of clustered, cast-iron columns surmounted by wrought-iron, stiff-leaf capitals and covered with steeply pitched, glass-tiled roofs. The Crystal Palace and London railway stations were all industrial precedents completed earlier, but the museum fulfils Acland's claim that gothic art would deal with iron and glass, and predates E-E Viollet-le-Duc's writings on the subject.

Ruskin was also closely involved with the construction; and Woodward's introduction of the Irish O'Shae brothers to carve the stonework using nature as their inspiration accorded with his beliefs. The brothers' lampooning of senior members of the university led to their dismissal, leaving the external decorative scheme incomplete.

ADDRESS Parks Road, opposite Museum Road
ACCESS Monday–Saturday 12.00–17.00; visible from Parks Road

Deane, Son and Woodward 1855–60

The University

Deane, Son and Woodward 1855–60

Oxford Union Society

The Union Society was founded as a debating club in 1823. In 1856 Benjamin Woodward of the Dublin practice Deane, Son and Woodward, at that time working on the University Museum (see page 118), was appointed to provide a purpose-built debating chamber. He designed a plain, oblong hall of red brick with pointed gothic windows, circular gallery windows and a very steep roof. The corners were angled, and a great marble fireplace was placed in the centre, with a chimney craftily ducted underfloor to an outside wall.

The painter Dante Gabriel Rossetti visited the building in 1857 and suggested that it needed decorating. He was one of the founders of the Pre-Raphaelite Brotherhood, whose cause had been championed by John Ruskin, at that time also closely involved with the University Museum. A group including William Morris and Edward Burne-Jones painted illustrations of the Arthurian legend directly on the walls around the gallery, but unfortunately the bright colours have now faded due to poor preparation of the painting surface. Morris also painted the roof, and then repainted it to a new design in 1875.

In 1863 a library echoing the form of the debating chamber was added alongside to a design by William Wilkinson, and in 1878 Alfred Waterhouse built a new debating chamber. The library is now housed in Woodward's original building. A new wing with gothic bay windows was added to designs by Mills and Thorpe in 1910–11.

ADDRESS St Michael's Street
ACCESS by appointment with librarian

B Woodward 1856–67, W Wilkinson 1863, A Waterhouse 1878

The University

B Woodward 1856–67, W Wilkinson 1863, A Waterhouse 1878

Examination Schools

With the Examination Schools, which he won in a limited competition in 1876, Sir Thomas G Jackson, who had worked in Sir George Gilbert Scott's office, turned his back decisively on the gothic revival, and introduced to Oxford a style of architecture hitherto unknown.

As inspiration for this, his first major building, he looked back eclectically to England in the sixteenth century. Jackson turned to that self-assured period of the English Renaissance that flowered in the reign of Elizabeth I and which was dominated by the architects Robert Smythson and his son John. The great prodigy houses of the period, such as Longleat, Wiltshire, and Burghley, Northamptonshire, were lit by rectangular windows divided by stone mullions and transoms, and were decorated with classical motifs derived mainly from France. The elevation to High Street closely follows this model and has similar windows rising through two storeys; the hall also has a hammerbeam roof.

Round the corner in Merton Street there is an open courtyard with a central three-storey clock tower frontispiece, which rather perversely turns out not to have an entrance door. This composition more specifically recalls Kirby Hall, Northamptonshire, although the upper windows have arched heads hinting at a slightly earlier period, while above runs a frieze of swags more reminiscent of Sir Christopher Wren.

It is only the steeply pitched roof that feels historically out of place in this fluent composition of tall, slender chimneys, corner turrets with ogee-shaped roofs, and shallow decorative pediments over gable windows, a style which soon became known as 'Anglo-Jackson'.

ADDRESS High Street and Merton Street
ACCESS none; visible from High Street and Merton Street

Sir Thomas G Jackson 1876–82

The University

Sir Thomas G Jackson 1876–82

Rhodes House

The will of the explorer and colonialist Cecil Rhodes endowed some 170 scholarships at the university for students from the United States, the British Empire and Germany, together with a new centre for their exclusive use.

Sir Herbert Baker, who had worked widely with Rhodes in South Africa, was commissioned by the trustees in 1929 to design the new building, Rhodes House. The result is a 'Cotswold Manor House', H-shaped in plan, with an Ionic entrance portico and classical rotunda, designed as a memorial to Rhodes Scholars who lost their lives in times of war, and placed rather incongruously between the two wings facing the road. Baker claimed that the composition fused a symbol of classical learning with the local vernacular, but the resulting marriage is curious. The interior is worth visiting for its fine timber fittings and spatial variety.

ADDRESS: South Parks Road
ACCESS: Monday–Friday 14.00–17.00

Sir Herbert Baker 1929

Sir Herbert Baker 1929

New Bodleian Library

The New Bodleian Library was commissioned in response to the ever increasing collections of the Bodleian Library. It was built to the designs of Sir Giles Gilbert Scott on a site at the corner of Broad Street and Parks Road. A tunnel under Broad Street and the Schools Quadrangle connects the old library with the new. A mechanical conveyor allows the transfer of books.

The library is of three storeys, in keeping with the surrounding buildings. The elevation to Broad Street is given a central emphasis by a slightly projecting bay, in line with the stack block behind, but curiously this does not mark the point of entry. The entrance is in fact towards the corner of Broad Street and Parks Road, and is marked by a strange imitation of a seventeenth-century portal. The stepping back of the elevation half way along its length, which creates a useless raised area between the pavement line and the building, is also difficult to explain.

The architectural language is an unpleasing version of stripped-down classicism, but with Georgian windows. The materials are rubble walls of Bladon stone with Clipsham stone dressings, which clad a steel and concrete structure. The stone detailing appears to allude to the architecture of Cotswold barns and farm houses rather than to the ashlar of the college buildings. The result, in this formal setting opposite Nicholas Hawksmoor's Clarendon Building (page 110), is incongruous to say the least. The architectural historian Howard Colvin has likened the design to 'a dinner jacket made of Harris Tweed'.

The University

ADDRESS Broad Street, opposite The Clarendon Building
ACCESS none; visible from Broad Street

Sir Giles Gilbert Scott 1937–40

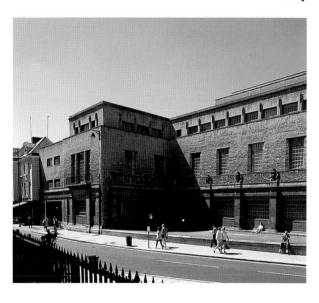

Sir Giles Gilbert Scott 1937–40

Law, English, and Economics & Statistics Libraries

This triumvirate of libraries was the first building in Oxford to be designed by Sir Leslie Martin. Formerly chief architect of the Greater London Council and in 1956 head of the Cambridge School of Architecture, Martin already had a reputation as one of the country's leading modern architects. Although the design post-dates his best work in Cambridge, particularly Harvey Court (1957–62), the library was Martin's first large public building and remains one of the best modern buildings in Oxford.

The formal arrangement is of three libraries of varying sizes placed around a core of shared lecture theatres and communal facilities. The building is entered on the first floor via a grand ceremonial external flight of steps which rises between the library blocks into the heart of the plan. This formal arrangement makes the user climb one storey to the entrance only to descend again to ground level to use the libraries.

The libraries take the form of 'blank boxes' within which the accommodation is arranged around central, top-lit atria. These boxes are expressed externally, although the terracing of the ancillary accommodation effectively buries them in the building mass. The materials of construction, horizontally stratified buff-coloured brickwork alternating with ribbon windows, are fluently employed in the modern idiom. The overall impression is of a low, horizontally layered building possessing a monumental and classical calm, a language arguably indebted to the late work of the Finnish architect Alvar Aalto.

ADDRESS St Cross Road
ACCESS none; visible from St Cross Road

Leslie Martin with St John Wilson, Hodgkinson and Lanham 1961–64

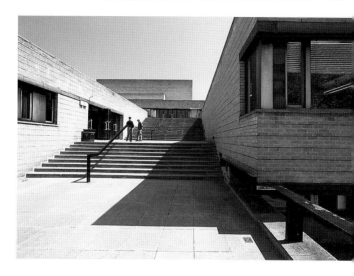

Leslie Martin with St John Wilson, Hodgkinson and Lanham 1961–

Mathematics Institute

The Mathematics Institute sits at the north end of St Giles' Street and was designed by Jack Lancaster, the University Surveyor. The building is designed in a solid British modernist tradition, owing much to the university work of Sir Leslie Martin at both Cambridge and Oxford (pages 128, 136 and 210).

The form of the building consists of two intersecting blocks placed at right angles to enclose a garden court behind an earlier stone wall. The larger block is set back from the street and is parallel with it, while the lower block projects towards the street and forms the entrance. Its height responds to the domestic scale of its medieval neighbours. The first floor is cantilevered out to provide shelter for the entrance. The brickwork at the ground-floor level is painted white, perhaps suggesting that the building mass above floats, or alluding to the white stucco of its neighbours. The datum level for the first floor takes its cue from the height of the pre-existing boundary wall. The Alvar Aalto-inspired architectural language of alternating horizontal bands of solid brickwork and fenestration is employed in a fluent and restrained manner. This building proves that the British modernist style of the 1960s was quite capable of producing successful contextual architecture.

ADDRESS St Giles' Street, north end
ACCESS none; visible from St Giles' Street

Jack Lancaster 1964–66

Jack Lancaster 1964–66

Zoology and Psychology Laboratories

During the late 1960s Sir Leslie Martin investigated building systems that would optimise the functional requirements of the building type, which in this case meant laboratories, while still allowing flexibility for change of use over time. Hence, the rather incongruous form and aesthetic of the Zoology and Psychology Laboratories, a building where contextual response appears not to have been on the agenda.

The building sits on a linear site between Parks Road and Balliol College playing fields, and is formally a series of repeating, stepped, concrete bays descending symmetrically either side of a linear service spine. The stepping section is reminiscent of a ziggurat or megastructure. The staircases are given separate formal expression and rise as towers above the body of the building.

Externally the building is divided into horizontal strata of alternating wall and window bands, which is very characteristic of Martin's work (page 128). The external materials are a mixture of precast and *in-situ* concrete, both made with white Portland stone, which are given horizontal or vertical shuttering marks depending on location. The main entrance is rather difficult to find, a recurring problem with buildings of the modern movement, but the internal public spaces are generous and carefully considered.

The same building form was originally intended to extend westwards in phases, but the proposal was abandoned in the 1980s when megastructures became unfashionable. The site now houses the unremarkable Virology Building by Architects Design Partnership (1981) and their Pharmacology Building (1992).

ADDRESS Parks Road
ACCESS none; visible from Parks Road and St Cross Road

Sir Leslie Martin with Douglas Lanham 1965–71

The University

The University

Sir Leslie Martin with Douglas Lanham 1965–71

Nuclear Physics and Engineering Laboratories

The buildings that make up the Oxford Science Area are mainly twentieth century and are largely of a disappointing architectural calibre. The exceptions are the Nuclear Physics and Engineering Laboratories, which are on the corner of Banbury and Keble Roads, and were designed by Arup Associates in a late-brutalist style. The most dramatic and symbolic feature of the scheme is the vast concrete fan-shaped tower attached to the north elevation, which contains a nuclear accelerator.

The brutalist label can be applied to both the organisational principles of design and to the use of materials. The design displays its internal organisation and structure on its exterior. A heavy concrete base containing plant and lecture theatres provides a solid podium upon which the laboratories and offices sit. The laboratories are arranged around three internal courtyards and are entered, rather unsatisfactorily, at first-floor level from an external walkway accessed via a wide staircase from Keble Road. This building was conceived as just the first phase of a much larger complex, which might explain the rather poor entrance sequence. The upper two storeys of laboratories are cantilevered over the podium storey and expressed as a light, glazed, box sitting on a concrete base.

The use of industrial materials in an honest (what you see is what you get) manner also marks the building as brutalist, although the obsessively careful design of the shuttered concrete and the highly refined detailing are contrary to the spirit of earlier brutalist buildings such as Le Corbusier's Unité d'habitation in Marseilles, France.

ADDRESS Banbury Road
ACCESS none; visible from Banbury Road and Keble Road

Ove Arup and Partners 1970, 1976

The University

Ove Arup and Partners 1970, 1976

University of Oxford Northern Residences

This mixed-use development of shops with flats above is the only built fragment of a larger scheme for the wholesale redevelopment of Wellington Square, a Victorian square south of Little Clarendon Street. The conservationists put a halt to the grand scheme in the 1970s because it required the demolition of important Victorian buildings.

The phase built forms both a street frontage to Little Clarendon Street, with arcaded shops on the ground floor, and the north range of Wellington Square. The linear form is stratified in a similar manner to Sir Leslie Martin's earlier Law, English, and Economics & Statistics Libraries (page 128), although in this case the materials are rather coarser – blockwork and in-situ concrete.

The façade to Little Clarendon Street steps down from four storeys to one in front of a continuous four-storey range as it moves away from Walton Street, perhaps not only as a gesture to give strength to the corner, but also to let light into the narrow street. The flats are accessed from closed, slightly projecting, staircase towers entered from a first-floor walkway on the Wellington Square elevation. Note the rather mannered stepping of the string course at each staircase. This elevation is slightly unsatisfactory as it was clearly designed as a modest composition, although in reality it is the prominent north elevation to Wellington Square.

Martin also designed the adjacent University Offices (1969–73) with a similar, but more institutional, aesthetic.

ADDRESS 25 Wellington Square
ACCESS none; visible from Wellington Square and Little Clarendon Street

Sir Leslie Martin with David Owers 1973–76

The University

The University

Sir Leslie Martin with David Owers 1973–76

Colleges: north-west of St Mary's

Balliol College, Chapel

In the early nineteenth century Balliol College secured intellectual primacy among the colleges under the long mastership of Richard Jenkyns, and to commemorate his time in office it resolved to build a new, and larger, chapel. The college employed William Butterfield as architect, who at that time was engaged on behalf of the Ecclesiologists in creating an appropriate setting for High Church ritual in London at All Saints, Margaret Street, now regarded as his masterpiece.

Butterfield decided to make the new chapel an exercise in combining thirteenth-century gothic with constructional polychrome banded stonework derived from cathedrals such as Orvieto and Siena in Tuscany, Italy. The chapel is substantially taller and wider than the one of 1522–29 that it replaced, and it dominates Front Quadrangle, a colourful contrast with James Wyatt's routine 1794 remodelling of the adjacent medieval ranges. The extra size was accommodated by allowing the chapel to project romantically into Garden Quadrangle, where Butterfield also built a slender turret, again banded. Inside, the polychromy continued, richly enhanced with alabaster and lavishly carved timber fittings.

The polychromy was not a success with Balliol or Trinity College, in whose Front Quadrangle the east gable is located. Toying with the idea of demolition, Balliol finally decided in 1937 to plaster over the interior of the chapel and substitute Butterfield's fittings with tame work in the classical mould.

Butterfield went on to design Keble College (page 156) in 1868, while Balliol employed Alfred Waterhouse around the same time, as a safer choice for the redevelopment of its Broad Street frontage.

ADDRESS Broad Street
ACCESS college open daily 14.00–17.00

William Butterfield 1856–57

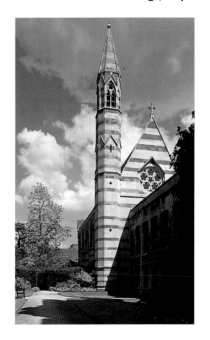

William Butterfield 1856–57

Balliol College, Bernard Sunley Building

The site chosen for Balliol College's new Senior Common Room was in the north-east corner of the Garden Quadrangle adjacent to Alfred Waterhouse's vast Victorian gothic hall, which would have been challenging for any architect in any period.

The new building appears to be a free-standing, two-storey pavilion, although it is in fact attached to the existing buildings at the rear. On the ground floor is a double-height common room overlooking the garden on two sides. In the basement is a lecture theatre, the roof of which is concealed externally by a sloping grass bank, and on the first floor is a reading room.

Working within the established 1960s modernist tradition of Oxford college architecture, championed by Powell and Moya, Sir Leslie Martin and the like, Oxford Architects Partnership attempted to design a building that drew on the context without resorting to stylistic plagiarism. Thus, the double-height stone columns to the common room, and the smaller bays above, are intended to exude a modern gothic spirit. Though a brave attempt, the new building sits slightly unhappily in the corner of the quadrangle, looking petite and out of scale next to Waterhouse's monumental hall.

ADDRESS Broad Street
ACCESS college open daily 14.00–17.00

Oxford Architects Partnership 1966–68

Colleges: north-west of St Mary's

Oxford Architects Partnership 1966–68

Brasenose College, Old Quadrangle

Brasenose College was founded in 1509 by William Smith, Bishop of Lincoln, and Sir Richard Sutton, a lawyer, on a site formerly occupied by Brasenose Hall. Old Quadrangle, the first part of the new college buildings, was designed as a unified composition, probably by a local master mason who drew on existing college quadrangles, such as at New College (page 234) and Merton College (page 294), as precedents.

The quadrangle is entered from Radcliffe Square through a four-storey gate tower with an embattled parapet and turret of 1512. Its façade is panelled and it has an oriel window flanked by two statue niches at high level. The quadrangle is bounded by four ranges of a consistent architectural language: two-storey ashlar façades with irregularly spaced, stone-mullioned windows with uncusped, round-headed arches and square hoods at ground level. The doorways also have square hoods. In addition, projecting first-floor bays are added intermittently. The north and west ranges were designed as two-storey residential buildings. Staircases serve two sets of rooms on each floor in the traditional Oxford manner. The east range contains the gateway tower and the Principal's lodgings immediately to the south. The south side has the buttery and hall, the latter with a bay window which lights the dais end and the busts of the founders. Internally the panelling is of 1684, and there is a mid-eighteenth-century plaster ceiling and fireplace.

A third storey in the roof was added to all four ranges early in the seventeenth century to provide extra accommodation for students. Known as 'cocklofts', the storey has large, gabled dormers giving the quadrangle a distinctive character. The sundial on the north range was added in 1719.

ADDRESS Radcliffe Square
ACCESS college open daily 10.00–11.30, 14.00–17.00

1509–18 and seventeenth century

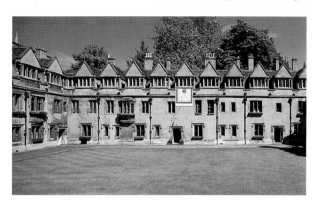

1509–18 and seventeenth century

Brasenose College, Chapel and Chapel Quadrangle

The small Chapel Quadrangle is entered from the south-east corner of Old Quadrangle and is formed by the seventeenth-century library to the east and the chapel to the south. The ranges are unified by a cloister that originally extended around the west side in front of the kitchen. In the eighteenth century the west part was removed and the remaining parts of the cloister enclosed.

John Jackson's design is an inventive mix of late gothic and early baroque styles; for example, the library windows, although traceried, also have pediments. The cloister detailing is also a mix, with attached pillars linked by a frieze with garlands in place of the expected gothic buttresses. The library interior and the façade to Radcliffe Square were remodelled by James Wyatt in 1782.

The chapel follows the New College T-plan (page 234) of five bays with an antechapel across the west end. Stylistically the chapel is just as exuberant as the east range. On the exterior, gothic windows are set between broad pilasters, with urns and crockets on the parapet. Yet the imposing antechapel portal has columns and a wide, open segmental pediment with a rectangular window – not at all gothic. The east end facing Radcliffe Square is also a mix of gothic window tracery and *cartouches*. Inside, the seventeenth-century gothic revival plaster fan vaulting and pendants are significant. Although the chapel was redecorated in the nineteenth century by Sir Thomas G Jackson, most of the interior fittings – the reredos, lectern, monuments and stained glass – are seventeenth century.

ADDRESS Radcliffe Square
ACCESS college open daily 10.00–11.30, 14.00–17.00

John Jackson (master mason) 1656–66

John Jackson (master mason) 1656–66

Exeter College, Chapel

Sir George Gilbert Scott, who designed the 1841 competition-winning Martyrs' Memorial (page 40), started work at Exeter College in 1854. He first designed the range to the west of the gate tower in Broad Street. Next came the gate tower itself, and the library. The chapel and rector's house followed in 1856, replacing the smaller seventeenth-century ones.

In the 1850s Scott and the members of the Ecclesiological Society had developed an interest in French thirteenth-century gothic architecture. This was sparked by George E Street's reports on his visits to France, and by E-E Viollet-le-Duc's introduction to the Society as an honorary member. Later, the style found expression in the entries submitted by members for the 1855 competition for a new cathedral at Lille in France. For his introductory address, Viollet-le-Duc spoke about his 1837 restoration of the Sainte Chapelle, a royal chapel which stands in a courtyard of the Palais de Justice in Paris. Possibly drawing a parallel with Oxford quadrangles, Scott, however inappropriately in the context, makes reference to the Sainte Chapelle in the plan and details of his Exeter chapel.

The chapel dominates the quadrangles it sits between, its height and verticality soaring above the residential ranges. As at the Sainte Chapelle a simple, apsidal plan is surrounded by full-height buttresses, each surmounted by a canopied saint, alternating with tall, pointed windows of geometric tracery. The steep roof is crowned by a slender spirelet or flèche, which is a French motif. The interior is High Victorian, with glass by Clayton and Bell, and stalls of 1884 by George F Bodley. There is also an 1890 Morris & Co. tapestry designed by Edward Burne-Jones.

ADDRESS Turl Street
ACCESS college open daily 14.00–17.00; admission charge

Sir George Gilbert Scott 1856–69

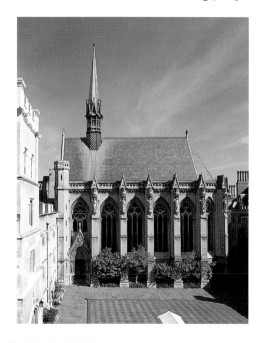

Colleges: north-west of St Mary's

Sir George Gilbert Scott 1856–69

Exeter College, Thomas Wood Building

Sir George Gilbert Scott's compact Margary Quadrangle, built to give Exeter College a frontage on Broad Street, had always been dark and unpleasant, overshadowed by his massive chapel (page 148). Shortly before 1964 the college decided to redevelop the adjoining block of buildings on the corner of Broad Street and Turl Street, pulling down Scott's intervening west range and building a new L-shaped corner to enlarge the quadrangle. Ground-floor shops facing the streets would increase college revenue, while there would be new student rooms above.

Lionel Brett worked in a modern Georgian-inspired idiom using flush-faced stonework with windows simply cut into the wall plane, their size determined by use. On Broad Street the smooth, clean stonework of his façade is a welcome twentieth-century contribution to the streetscape. The shops, at half basement and mezzanine levels, are visually separated from the residential accommodation above by a black line, which is a clerestory lighting the mezzanine, while to relate to Scott's work, Brett extended his pitched roof above the new façade.

In Turl Street the building is subdivided into three sections, responding to the smaller scale of the street: the return of the Broad Street frontage, then a lower section, and finally a six-storey tower in the form of a canted bay, which echoes the gate tower of the college along the street.

Inside the enlarged Margary Quadrangle, the new tower is the same height as the chapel. The building is further articulated by glazed stair towers, and its clean lines are a good foil to Scott's High Victorian gothic.

ADDRESS Broad Street and Turl Street
ACCESS college open daily 14.00–17.00; admission charge

Lionel Brett and Francis Pollen 1964

Lionel Brett and Francis Pollen 1964

Green College, Radcliffe Observatory

The Radcliffe Observatory was commissioned by the Radcliffe Trustees to house the university observatory. Henry Keene was approached for a design in 1772, but it received public criticism, and the trustees appointed James Wyatt instead to produce a new design. Funds were only released gradually, and the building was not completed till 1794.

Wyatt was an experienced architect who worked in many styles and had already built the neo-classical Christ Church Canterbury Quadrangle (1773–83) (page 280). However, the use of the Greek revival for the observatory was new for both Wyatt and for Oxford. His design rejected observatory precedents, such as Sir Christopher Wren's Royal Observatory at Greenwich (1675), preferring to use the ancient Greek Tower of the Winds in Athens as inspiration for its form. Thus, a canted square tower projects from a two-storey base with one-storey wings attached. The elevational treatment is plain and restrained. The sculptor John Bacon RA carved the low relief and delicate external decoration. The medallions over the windows at first-floor level depict signs of the zodiac, and each face of the tower has a frieze carved with reliefs of the named Winds. Hercules and Atlas support the globe on the apex of the roof.

Internally there are three major rooms. The ground floor has an entrance hall, the first floor a *piano nobile*, and the top room a double-height observatory with a circular gallery at an intermediate level and tall windows for viewing the night sky through telescopes.

The observatory is no longer in use and now forms part of Green College.

ADDRESS Woodstock Road
ACCESS apply to domestic bursar

James Wyatt 1776–94

James Wyatt 1776–94

Jesus College, Front Quadrangle

The residential part of Front Quadrangle's east range, which faces Turl Street, was built soon after Jesus College's foundation in 1571. It has twice been remodelled: first in 1756 when a Palladian gateway was built, and then in 1854 when the gate tower was heightened and the elevations to Turl Street and Market Street given their present gothic appearance by John C Buckler and Charles A Buckler.

The remainder of the quadrangle was built between 1617 and 1621 with simple, square-headed windows with continuous hood moulds and string courses. The hall, with three large, square-headed windows, faces the gateway, and the Principal's lodgings and chapel are on the north side. The attic storey of the lodgings was given an embattled parapet in 1733–41 and the rest of the quadrangle was embattled in 1815, giving it its present appearance.

In 1636 the chapel was extended one bay east to Turl Street and one bay west, retaining the simple Jacobean gothic tracery. In 1864 it was remodelled internally, and a new chancel arch was built by George Edmund Street.

Inner Quadrangle, beyond Front Quadrangle, was built between 1635 and 1713 to a uniform design, using the small gables also used at University College (page 310) by the same mason. These were also added to the west face of the hall for uniformity.

ADDRESS Turl Street, west side
ACCESS college open daily 14.00–16.30

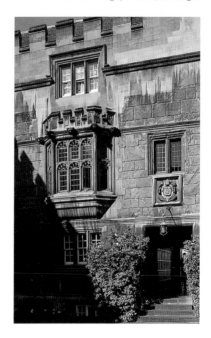

Sixteenth and seventeenth centuries

Keble College

Keble College was founded by public subscription in memory of John Keble, whose 1833 sermon on national apostasy and popular religious writings helped to found the High-Church Oxford Movement, whose leading architect was William Butterfield. Keble, the first new college for over 250 years, was meant for poor students and the sons of clerics.

The college was to break with Oxford tradition in more ways than one. The site chosen was isolated from the university and city centre, where land was scarce. Butterfield's principal use of red brick instead of stone for the college buildings was unprecedented. New again was the arrangement of rooms off corridors, rather than stairs, to reduce the need for college servants. The buildings present a unity of quintessentially High Victorian gothic style, although by the 1870s Butterfield's anti-puritanical polychromy, stone banding, diaper patterning and use of thirteenth-century English motifs had been abandoned by younger architects.

The two quadrangles, Liddon, with its sunken lawn, and Pusey, are named after Oxford Movement luminaries. The residential ranges have a horizontal emphasis, punctuated by tall chimneys and gables, and a directness of detailing. By contrast, the chapel, diagonally opposite the enormous first-floor hall, appropriately soars over Liddon Quadrangle, its windows only starting above the level of the adjacent roofs. It is a *tour de force* of verticality, pattern and ornament, crowned with pinnacles. Inside, the pews defer properly to the altar by facing east, another break with collegiate tradition. Unlike Butterfield's Balliol College chapel (page 140), the exuberant use of marbles, mosaics and patterning inside has been preserved as built.

ADDRESS Parks Road
ACCESS open daily 14.00–17.00

William Butterfield 1868–82

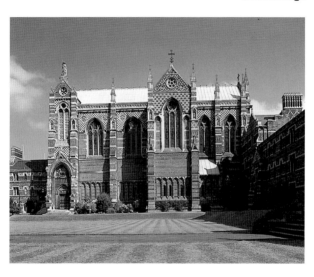

Colleges: north-west of St Mary's

William Butterfield 1868–82

Keble College, De Breyne and Hayward Buildings

Keble College had altered little from William Butterfield's High Victorian gothic style until the late 1960s when Ahrends Burton and Koralek were commissioned to design a new building with student residences, fellows' rooms and communal facilities. ABK followed Butterfield's strategy by placing the building around the perimeter of the site. The new building runs along the Blackhall Road boundary to the west and the Museum Road boundary to the south. But there the similarity with Butterfield ends. The ABK building is designed as one room deep, containing student rooms in pairs on each floor, which are served by communal stairs accessed from a ground-floor cloister. This is unlike the Butterfield model of rooms off a corridor, and reverts to the usual Oxford plan.

The building wraps around a small quadrangle at the south end, snakes along its length and terminates in the common room at the north end. The architectural language is simple and monumental. The building presents itself as a battered, fortress-like high wall to the outside world. This sheer buff brick wall is modulated into bays by recessed vertical glass slots giving light to the enclosed staircase towers. The structure is of brick load-bearing cross walls. Within the college the façade is a single cascading glass wall, whose skirt covers a ground-floor semi-sunken open cloister. The result is a delight. The new building sits quietly next to Butterworth's polychromy – two quite different architectural styles happily co-existing.

ADDRESS Parks Road
ACCESS college open daily 14.00–17.00; visible from Blackhall Road and Museum Road

Ahrends Burton and Koralek 1969–77

Ahrends Burton and Koralek 1969–77

Keble College, Arco Building

In 1991 Rick Mather Architects won an open competition for a new residential building for a site on the north side of Keble College Fellows' Garden, along the boundary to Keble Road.

The new building extends the building line and formal massing of the residential range to the east of William Butterfield's High Victorian gothic chapel (page 156). The height of the new five-storey building is kept down by placing seminar rooms on the lower-ground floor. By gently raking down the garden Mather provided good natural light and a pleasant view for these rooms. The façade to Keble Road is rather austere in character with its single plane of red brickwork, the square window openings kept within strict horizontal bands, and clipped eaves. The garden elevation is more interesting. The façade steps out one-third of the way along its length and then rakes back on plan in response to the internal circulation, which appears to force the plan apart in the centre. This curving façade, which is raised above the seminar rooms on pilotis, is expressed as a plane punctured by small, regularly spaced, triangular bay windows. The external cladding on all four sides is of hand-made red bricks. Less high than, normal bricks they are laid in Roman bond variously in horizontal and vertical panels.

The building is entered from the ground-floor level via a bridge, the route either descending to the seminar rooms or ascending within a top-lit atrium, which is pointed and curved in plan, to student rooms and a roof terrace. The design of the circulation is, like the rest of the building, refreshing in its use of the modernist aesthetic.

ADDRESS Parks Road
ACCESS college open daily 14.00–17.00; visible from Keble Road and Blackhall Road

Rick Mather Architects 1995

Colleges: north-west of St Mary's

Rick Mather Architects 1995

Lincoln College, Front Quadrangle

Front Quadrangle took its present form between 1427 and 1429, shortly after Lincoln College's foundation by Richard Fleming, Bishop of Lincoln, in whose diocese Oxford fell. As now, the quadrangle was built with two storeys, but practically nothing remains of its original appearance. The gate tower and west range, the north range, including a chapel and library, and the hall and kitchen to the east were all complete by 1437; the old rector's lodging south of the hall by c.1465; and the south range in 1479.

In the early seventeenth century a new quadrangle was started to the south of Front Quadrangle, and in 1629–31 a new chapel was built on its south side. Despite its late date, the chapel is in the Perpendicular gothic style with a timber roof. The glass is all contemporary with the chapel, and the screen is c.1675. The old chapel in Front Quadrangle was converted to fellows' rooms.

In the eighteenth century the windows in Front Quadrangle were enlarged and fitted with sashes, the stonework refaced and a parapet added; in 1824 the entire elevations along Turl Street and Brasenose Lane were rebuilt, replacing the small, irregular medieval windows with evenly spaced ones with a battlemented parapet above. There is thus little left of the quadrangle's fifteenth-century appearance.

ADDRESS Turl Street
ACCESS college open Monday–Saturday 14.00–17.00, Sunday 11.00–17.00

Fifteenth, seventeenth and nineteenth centuries

Fifteenth, seventeenth and nineteenth centuries

Lincoln College, Library (formerly All Saints Church)

The parish church of All Saints, built anew after the spire of the original medieval church collapsed in 1699, is a fine example of early eighteenth-century church architecture. A single cubic volume without aisles or chancel, and well lit on three sides, it was ideally suited to church practices of the time and owed much to Sir Christopher Wren's church designs for London following the great fire. An early design, now in the RIBA Drawings Collection, showed a single entrance portico in the middle of the High Street side, (although this was moved to alongside the tower and another portico introduced on Turl Street). The thorough and learned classicism of this design inescapably points to Dean Henry Aldrich as the architect.

The rusticated western tower, clearly visible down the length of Turl Street, was completed before Aldrich died in 1710, unlike his delicate steeple, loosely modelled on Wren's St Mary-le-Bow. Nicholas Hawksmoor subsequently produced a revised design, elongating the peristyle and surmounting it with a dome. As built in 1718–20 by William Townesend, the steeple retains Aldrich's balustrade, uses Hawksmoor's peristyle, and surmounts this by a steeple that is plainer than Aldrich's. It is a fine contribution to Oxford's celebrated skyline.

In 1975 All Saints was converted to a library for Lincoln College to a design by Robert Potter. The floor level was raised to create a basement bookstore, and the church fittings, many of which had been replaced by Sir Thomas G Jackson in his 1896 restoration, were reconfigured in the upper reading area.

ADDRESS High Street, north side
ACCESS none; visible from Turl Street and High Street

Dean Henry Aldrich 1701–10, Robert Potter 1975

Dean Henry Aldrich 1701–10, Robert Potter 1975

Nuffield College

Nuffield College was founded in 1937 by William Morris, the Oxford car manufacturer, as a graduate college for students of the social sciences. The trustees appointed an expatriate architect, Austin Harrison, who brought in T S Barnes and R P S Hubbard to assist him, to design the new college for a site on the disused Oxford Canal terminal basin. A preliminary proposal, with a formal beaux-arts plan and architecture with distinctive Mediterranean influences, was rejected by Morris (then Viscount Nuffield), who considered it 'un-English'. Harrison subsequently produced a second, less formal, design inspired by Cotswold vernacular architecture. The foundation stone was laid in 1949, but the building was not completed until 1956.

The layout of the new college is loosely based on the Oxford college typology, with two adjoining principal quadrangles entered through a gate house from New Road. The plan retains the two cardinal axes of the first scheme, but they no longer terminate in foci, resulting in a less formal aesthetic. Yet the quadrangles themselves are laid out in a strict geometrical manner, with lawns, stone paths, herbaceous borders and pools.

Harrison's vernacular style meant long two-storey ranges with gable ends, ashlar walls, windows with stone mullions and leaded lights, and steeply pitched Cotswold stone roofs with hipped dormers and chimneys. The result is competent but dull. There remains just a hint of the Mediterranean flavour of the earlier design in the stone carving of the principal doorway arches. The nine-storey library tower has a quite different aesthetic to the rest of the college and was built last, in 1956.

ADDRESS New Road
ACCESS Monday–Saturday 09.00–17.00, Sunday 10.00–17.00

Harrison, Barnes and Hubbard 1937–56

Colleges: north-west of St Mary's

Harrison, Barnes and Hubbard 1937–56

St Anne's College, Wolfsen and Rayne Buildings

The 1960s was a time of great expansion for colleges generally, which necessitated new student accommodation. Howell Killick Partridge and Amis were commissioned by St Anne's College, a recently founded women's college, to look at the possibility of building new student rooms as a phased development in the college grounds. The architects devised a series of six small freestanding residential blocks placed in a picturesque snaking manner on the edge of a newly formed lake, located between them and Banbury Road. Only two of the towers of this grand plan were built, the Wolfsen and Rayne Buildings.

Each block has a simple rectangular plan, which gently bows outwards at the centre, with a single band of student rooms located each side of a central corridor. The corridor contains a central circular stair, separate escape stairs, toilets, stores, etc. The blocks are four storeys high, and divided horizontally in a tripartite manner; a recessed base, a middle divided into seven bays, and a plain top. Although the structure is of load-bearing brickwork, the exterior aesthetic is provided by cladding; vertical bays of precast concrete panels rise through three storeys and are faced in granite aggregate. The heavy modelling of the middle band is achieved by giving each study-bedroom a balcony, which is individually expressed on the exterior as a large opening with projecting inwardly tapering sides. It could be argued that the language is a little over-wrought, but the combination of curving forms and modest scale results in buildings that sit very comfortably in their landscape setting.

ADDRESS Woodstock Road
ACCESS apply to porter's lodge

Howell Killick Partridge and Amis 1968

Howell Killick Partridge and Amis 1968

St Anthony's College, Hall and Common Rooms

St Anthony's College was founded as a new postgraduate college in 1950, and took over the grounds and austere Victorian Early English gothic revival buildings designed by Charles Buckeridge (1866–88) for the Convent of the Most Holy and Undivided Trinity. In 1970 the college commissioned Howell Killick Partridge and Amis to design a new building with social spaces for the college, primarily a hall and common rooms.

The design takes the form of a large pavilion sitting in the college gardens. The pavilion has a striking imagery: repeated bays of double-height white precast concrete panels with hooded window openings are raised on a slender concrete frame, reminiscent of *art brut* sculptures of the 1950s. The building is entered from the east or west, and is organised on four floors: the basement has a wine store and boiler house; the ground floor an entrance lobby, three private dining rooms and a buttery; the first floor a double-height hall and kitchens; and the second floor two common rooms and a gallery overlooking the hall. The formal plan has two equal rectangles symmetrically disposed about a north–south circulation axis, which is terminated by two staircase towers. In plan the building is simple, but the section is complex, and a carefully planned circulation sequence joins together a spatially varied set of rooms. The double-height hall with its precast, post-tensioned diagrid ceiling is of particular note.

The architectural language of 'building as kit of parts' is also a thematic development of the architect's earlier Wolfsen and Rayne Buildings at St Anne's College (page 168).

ADDRESS Woodstock Road
ACCESS none; visible from Woodstock Road

Howell Killick Partridge and Amis 1970

Howell Killick Partridge and Amis 1970

St Cross College, Richard Blackwell Quadrangle (Pusey House)

St Cross College, named after the former parish school in which it started life in 1965, moved to Pusey House in 1981. Pusey House was founded in 1884 as an Anglican theological centre, and named after Edward Pusey, a leading member of the High-Church Oxford Movement. It retains the use of the chapel and the theological library, while St Cross College uses the other buildings. In 1993 the college extended into the garden with a new hall designed by the Oxford Architects Partnership.

Richard Blackwell Quadrangle, recently renamed after a benefactor of the college, is all twentieth-century gothic by Temple Moore. Its domestic scale is enhanced by a narrow window module, shallow bays, a battlemented parapet and small dormers. With its tall chimneys it could easily be mistaken for a medieval hall, clumsily reroofed with red tiles. There is no traditional gate tower, however, and the offset entrance from St Giles' Street, linking to a cloister-like corridor leading to the chapel, is delightfully small in scale.

The chapel, with its very solid-looking tower, dominates the quadrangle without detracting from it. Inside, the chapel is divided into a five-bay nave and three-bay chancel by a stone screen. The stone vaulting, narrow wall passage and other details are all inventive. The 1937 east window, gilded ciborium and altar setting are by Sir Ninian Comper, and they introduce a note of *cinquecento* extravagance.

ADDRESS St Giles' Street, west side
ACCESS apply to domestic bursar

Temple Moore 1911–14

Temple Moore 1911–14

St John's College, Canterbury Quadrangle

In 1629 William Laud was made Chancellor of the university. Shortly afterwards, he decided to finance new accommodation behind the medieval quadrangle of the college where he had been President. A new free-standing library had already been completed in the garden in 1601, and it was decided to incorporate this into the south range of a new quadrangle. Work progressed on the new residential range opposite the library, aligned to avoid the east window of the existing chapel, and on the garden side to the east a colonnade was built linking this to the library.

The masons were discharged in 1633 and John Jackson, a London mason, was hired instead. Adam Browne, who had already worked for Laud, was employed to prepare a drawing and model. The project had already grown to include a west colonnade behind Front Quadrangle, with a long gallery above to serve the President's lodging, and a second library had been built above the east colonnade. Browne must have been responsible for the colonnades' Italianate style and the design of the opposing pair of mannerist frontispieces with their prominent segmental pediments, which transformed this into the grandest and most sophisticated scheme of its time in Oxford. This exuberant design contrasts strangely with the just-completed gothic fan-vaulted gateways, Tudor gothic windows and oriel windows overlooking the garden, which at that time was laid out formally as a series of walled compartments.

Laud commissioned Hubert Lesueur to cast bronze statues of Charles I and Queen Henrietta Maria. These were in place for a royal visit in 1636, just four years before Laud's downfall.

ADDRESS St Giles' Street, east side
ACCESS college open daily 13.00–17.00

Adam Browne 1631–36

St John's College, The Beehives

The Beehives is of historical importance because it was the first post-war college building in Oxford to employ the architectural language of the modern movement. The building completes the east range of North Quadrangle, and consists of three rows of two-storey tessellated hexagonal linked pavilions. The outer rows of the pavilions contain study-bedrooms and face either the courtyard or the garden. The sandwiched row of hexagons contains staircases and service rooms. The three internal staircases are lit with hexagonal lanterns, which also provide modulation of the roof line. The design is a wilful, and not wholly successful, attempt at shoe-horning accommodation into a preconceived formal geometry. The entrance from North Quadrangle appears an afterthought and is most unsatisfactory. The materials used for the building, ashlar and slate, mirror those used in the surrounding buildings, and were meant to assimilate the building into its context. However incongruous the hexagonal forms, they are distinctive and memorable, and have resulted in the building being affectionately known as 'The Beehives'.

ADDRESS St Giles' Street
ACCESS college open daily 13.00–17.00

Colleges: north-west of St Mary's

Architects Co-Partnership 1958

Colleges: north-west of St Mary's

Architects Co-Partnership 1958

St John's College, Sir Thomas White Building

The Sir Thomas White Building is arguably the best of its period in Oxford. Designed by the multidisciplinary firm Arup Associates, it provides 156 graduate and undergraduate rooms.

The formal arrangement is of a four-storey, L-shaped block of eleven pavilions linked by staircase towers forming the north and east ranges of the landscaped college garden. To the rear the north range faces Lamb's Passage where the concrete frame straddles the existing stone boundary wall sensitively. The ground floor on the garden side is colonnaded, gives access to the staircases serving the study-bedrooms, and is clearly an attempt to reinterpret the typology of the Oxford cloister. Each pavilion is defined by a precast concrete exoskeleton, the proportions of which reflect the size of individual rooms. This open-frame structure alternates with solid stone staircase towers to provide the dominant rhythm and scale of the building. The roof line is modulated by the frame verticals and projecting staircase towers. The layering of the study-bedroom façades, with glass sitting behind the frame structure, and timber screens in turn sitting behind the glass, gives an additional fine, more intimate texture. The palette of materials – bush-hammered concrete for the frame, ashlar for the staircases and hardwood generally – together with impeccable detailing, gives the impression of solidity and quality.

The building's architecture demonstrates an all-round sensibility rarely seen in work of that date. It is a subtle essay in contextualism, which additionally develops the building type and demonstrates a sophisticated architectural language.

ADDRESS St Giles' Street
ACCESS college open daily 13.00–17.00; visible from Lamb's Passage

Arup Associates 1975

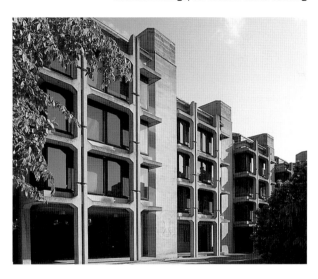

Arup Associates 1975

St John's College, Garden Quadrangle

Although the Garden Quadrangle building had a similar brief to the earlier modernist Sir Thomas White Building (page 178), the architectural language employed is very different. The strong prospect towers, plain ranges and large expanses of window allude to sixteenth-century Elizabethan buildings, such as Hardwick Hall, Derbyshire. The site for the new building is in the north-east corner of the college grounds, the building forming a new northern boundary to the gardens.

The design has great similarity in schematic concept and detail to the practice's earlier Bowra Building at Wadham College (page 262). The St John's College site and brief was larger than at Wadham, hence the generous first-floor quadrangle with new buildings on four sides. The south side is almost open to the garden except for two low towers, while on the other three sides the towers and staircases form a continuous, but modulated, wall of building. Communal rooms and car parking are placed at ground-floor level and form the podium for the first-floor quadrangle which gives access to blocks of student rooms. The blocks are expressed as clerestoried, brick prospect towers sitting on the podium, with staircases infilling between. The quadrangle is punctured by two circular lanterns and a large central circular open well, allowing light to enter.

The architectural language is more mannered than the Bowra Building. Stone dressings are used in excess, and there is even classical rustication at podium level, which alludes to the work of Sir John Soane. The overall impression is of a building rather weighed down by monumental detailing, which nevertheless exudes quality and opulence.

ADDRESS St Giles' Street
ACCESS college open daily 13.00–17.00

MacCormac Jamieson and Prichard 1993

MacCormac Jamieson and Prichard 1993

St Peter's College

St Peter's Hall was founded in 1928 and became a college in 1961. Its site is bounded on the west by the line of the old city wall, and is raised, probably on spoil dug from the castle moat (page 18).

Entry is through Linton House, built in 1797 in the Georgian style as the offices of the Oxford Canal Company, and used as a rectory from 1829. Opposite are the Main Buildings of red brick and stone in a William and Mary style, designed by R Fielding Dodd in the 1930s. To the right the concrete Latner Building of 1971–72 is by Kenneth Stevens. The chapel is an early work by Basil Champneys, his 1874 rebuilding in the gothic style of the parish church of St Peter-le-Bailey.

South Quadrangle consists principally of two buildings. Facing New Inn Hall Street is the converted Central School for Girls, designed in 1899–1901 by Leonard Stokes in an Arts and Crafts manner. The side facing the quadrangle, with its large gabled classroom windows, tall chimneys and white-painted belfry, has been partly obscured by insensitive new work at ground level. Opposite is a residential block of 1987–88 by Chamberlain Powell Bon and Woods (illustrated). This establishes yet another architectural language for the college, and a focal point in the form of a glazed stair tower.

The master's lodgings are to the west of the site, across Bulwark Lane and visible from New Road, in a forceful Greek revival building. The lodgings were built in 1827–29 by Richard Tawney as the new Oxford Canal Company offices to serve the canal basin, on the site of which Nuffield College (page 166) now stands.

ADDRESS New Inn Hall Street, west side
ACCESS open daily 09.00–dusk

Chamberlain Powell Bon and Woods 1987–88 and others

Chamberlain Powell Bon and Woods 1987–88 and others

Somerville College, Fry and Vaughan Buildings

As a response to increasing student numbers in the 1960s Somerville College commissioned Arup Associates to design a development of shops, graduate student residences and communal facilities on an infill site on the south side of Garden Quadrangle bounding Little Clarendon Street.

The formal composition places two residential blocks, one following the street line and the other set back slightly, on top of a one-storey podium containing shops and a rear entrance to the college. From Little Clarendon Street the podium reads as a series of flat, concrete arches, at right angles to the street, supported on columns at the front to form a colonnade to the shops. A brick wall, rather weakly detailed to allude to castellations, forms the parapet of the podium and attempts to maintain the street line.

The two residential blocks are of four storeys above the podium level, the lowest of which contains communal areas for the students. On each of the upper floors there are eight student rooms accessed from a wide, double-sided corridor which has the vertical circulation and service areas at each end.

The dominant aesthetic is the precast concrete exoskeleton of the residential blocks, its cell-like imagery reflecting the 1960s' interest in biological forms. The weathering layer, of glass and precast concrete panels housed in a delicate concrete framework, is set well back from the outer framework and provides privacy for the rooms, giving the overall impression of a box within a box.

ADDRESS Woodstock Road, south end
ACCESS college open daily 14.00–17.30; visible from Little Clarendon Street

Arup Associates 1965

Arup Associates 1965

Somerville College, Wolfsen Building

The Wolfsen Building was Arup Associates' second commission from Somerville College, the first being the Fry and Vaughan Buildings (page 184). The brief was again to provide student residences, but this time the site was at the far side of the Garden Quadrangle, between the Elizabethan-style West Building (1886–94) and the neo-Georgian Penrose Building (1927), with the high stone wall along Walton Street as its rear boundary.

The Wolfsen Building fills the gap between the West and Penrose Buildings with a five-bay, four-storey, concrete-framed pavilion, flanked by solid brick staircase towers with raking tops. The brickwork of the towers and the ground-floor screen beneath the central block are obviously meant to relate to the building's neighbours. On the Walton Street side the form aligns with the existing building line, sitting quietly behind the high stone wall. This elevation repeats the garden façade, curiously taking no account of the different aspect.

The architectural language is completely different to the Fry and Vaughan Buildings, although it is still within the British modernist idiom. Here, full-height, frameless oriel windows, one for each room, give the impression of being slung from a precast concrete frame. The frame has slender concrete posts that project above the roof line in the manner of pinnacles, and forward-projecting beams which run back through the building at each floor level. The effect is altogether more delicate than Arup Associates' earlier work.

ADDRESS Woodstock Road, south end
ACCESS college open daily 14.00–17.30; visible from Walton Street

Arup Associates 1968

Colleges: north-west of St Mary's

Arup Associates 1968

Trinity College, Garden Quadrangle

The basis of Garden Quadrangle was established by Sir Christopher Wren in 1665 when he built its first building, but the three-storey open quadrangle only acquired its final form in 1802.

Early in his career as an architect, while the Sheldonian Theatre (page 106) was under construction, Wren produced a drawing for a new, free-standing, residential block. Although he wanted it to be built in the garden, it was actually constructed a short distance to the north of the college, which consisted just of the medieval Durham Quadrangle. Wren's simple drawing shows a plain, symmetrical, two-storey classical building with a mansard roof and dormer windows. There is a doorway each side of a central bay, which steps forward and is crowned with a pediment. The present north range embodies Wren's building.

In 1682 an identical range was built on the west side of the quadrangle, joining Wren's block to the outside of the medieval quadrangle, and giving Garden Quadrangle its present plan form – a three-sided court open to the garden on the east, a plan similar to the exactly contemporary Garden Quadrangle at New College (page 238). Forty-six years later the master mason William Townesend was employed to reface the south side of the quadrangle, making all three sides uniform with Wren's original block. In 1802 the quadrangle took on its present appearance: the mansard roofs and pediments were removed, a third storey added, and the cross-shaped windows replaced with sliding sashes.

ADDRESS Broad Street, north side
ACCESS college open daily 10.30–12.00, 14.00–17.00

1665, 1682, 1728 and 1802

1665, 1682, 1728 and 1802

Trinity College, Chapel

Sadly, the architect of this late seventeenth-century classical masterpiece is not known, though doubtless he was paying homage to Sir Christopher Wren, whose Sheldonian Theatre (page 106) was then nearing completion across Broad Street. Dean Henry Aldrich may have been involved, and Wren, who liked the design, was consulted on only minor details, including the windows, cornice and pinnacles. Despite the anonymity of its authorship, Trinity College chapel has a dignified classical authority. The master mason was either Bartholomew Peisley I or his son.

The building's form recalls the college's medieval gate tower and the adjacent chapel it was built to replace, but is treated instead as a unified architectural whole, with the gate tower doubling as a bell tower for the chapel. Perhaps surprisingly, the chapel is still entered from the quadrangle rather than axially from beneath the tower, emphasising that it is necessary to enter the college before entering the chapel.

Dr Bathurst, President of the college from 1664 to 1704, gave money for the shell, and the fitout was financed by subscription, resulting in one of Oxford's best baroque interiors. Again, the designer is not known, but the master carpenter was Arthur Frogley, who also worked at St Edmund Hall (page 254). The juniper veneer of the richly decorated screen, stalls and reredos has a rich lustre, while the pearwood swags may have been carved by Grinling Gibbons. Only the late nineteenth-century glass is discordant. The panelled enclosures flanking the altar house the mid-sixteenth-century founder's tomb, reset from the medieval chapel on the north side and opposite the President's pew with its own external entrance.

ADDRESS Broad Street, north side
ACCESS college open daily 10.30–12.00, 14.00–17.00

Seventeenth century

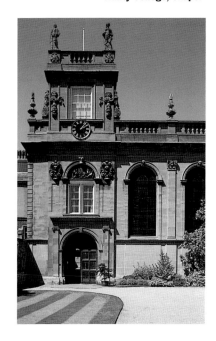

Seventeenth century

Trinity College, Cumberbatch Quadrangle and Blackwell's Bookshop

As a consequence of the growth of the book trade in the 1970s, Blackwell's Bookshop wished to expand its Broad Street premises. The land surrounding the shop was owned by Trinity College, and together they devised a mutually beneficial development: an expansion of the bookshop and new residential accommodation for the college. Maguire and Murray devised an ingenious infill development at the rear of the existing shop, which provided Blackwell's with a vast underground area to house their science department, on top of which two new quadrangles were formed by placing a new residential building between Sir Thomas G Jackson's 'New Building' (1881–82) and the south end of the college library. In addition, a four-storey pavilion was designed facing the college garden and adjoining the north end of the library. This contained more student rooms and a ground-floor assembly room.

This development was perhaps the first college architecture in Oxford to take cues for its language from the surrounding vernacular of the medieval houses rather than from the high architecture of the colleges. The architects did not undertake a pastiche, but rather attempted to evoke the intimate scale, rich forms and soft materials of the vernacular. Hence the language of asymmetry, projecting timber bays, brickwork and pitched roofs. However, within this gentle architectural language there is an underlying formality and rationality in plan and section that sets the building firmly within the modernist tradition.

ADDRESS Broad Street
ACCESS college open daily 10.30–12.00, 14.00–17.00; bookshop open Monday and Wednesday–Saturday 09.00–18.00, Tuesday 09.30–18.00, Sunday 11.00–17.00

Maguire and Murray 1968

Maguire and Murray 1968

Worcester College, Main Quadrangle, South Range

The South Range of Worcester College's Main Quadrangle predates the foundation of the college (1714), and was originally built as the residences for Gloucester College, a Benedictine monastic college founded in 1283. The range, a two-storey ashlar building with steeply pitched stone-tiled roofs, is all that survives of the medieval college.

The building was designed as a series of self-contained lodgings, or *camerae*, so that the Benedictines could let sets of rooms to individual monasteries, each monastery being responsible for the upkeep of its own *camera*. The individual units can be clearly distinguished from the way the elevation steps slightly at each party wall, and they may have been built incrementally. The doorways to the *camerae* are adorned with trefoils, quatrefoils or foliage in the spandrels, and have coats of arms above which represent the original tenant. The position and nature of the fenestration have been considerably altered over the years, and the original windows may have had arches and cusping.

Internally each *camera* occupied two storeys connected by a winding staircase, each storey being divided into smaller rooms by lightweight partitioning. The present buildings have been much altered internally but there are original moulded ceiling beams and a wagon roof, with moulded ribs and plain blocks at intersections, in the easternmost *camera*.

The rear of the range has been greatly altered over the years, although the chimney breast at the west end, originally serving the kitchen, is probably fifteenth century. The adjacent Pump Quadrangle is also medieval.

ADDRESS Worcester Street
ACCESS college open daily: term 14.00–18.00; vacation 09.00–12.00, 14.00–18.00

Fifteenth century

Fifteenth century

Worcester College, Main Quadrangle, Central Block and North Range

Worcester College was founded in 1714 under the will of Sir Thomas Cookes, on the site of the medieval Gloucester College. Although the buildings remained, Cookes left money for a new 'ornamental pile'; only the South Range of the original quadrangle was retained (page 194). The new Central Block and North Range were built between 1720 and 1791.

The design of the Central Block is attributed to Dr George Clarke, architect and college benefactor, who was assisted by Nicholas Hawksmoor. However, the designs were probably altered by the master mason William Townesend. The three-storey ashlar block, with a central entrance and bold three-storey projecting wings containing the chapel and hall, was designed as the college entrance. The recessed main block was built first, forming the East Range of the Main Quadrangle and housing a cloister, giving access to a hall, chapel and long library on the first floor. The robust, dignified composition of the elevation to the quadrangle makes it one of the finest classical façades in Oxford. The hall and chapel were not completed until 1784 and 1791 respectively, accounting for their more delicate style. Their interiors were decorated by James Wyatt in a refined neo-classical style, the chapel being redecorated in a High Victorian style in 1863–64 by William Burges. The residential North Range is a symmetrical three-storey classical block, with the central three bays projecting slightly and surmounted by a pediment. The design of the eastern half is attributed to Clarke, while the western part and the adjoining provost's lodgings are attributed to Henry Keene.

ADDRESS Worcester Street
ACCESS college open daily: term 14.00–18.00; vacation 09.00–12.00, 14.00–18.00

Dr George Clarke, Nicholas Hawksmoor and Henry Keene 1720–91

Dr George Clarke, Nicholas Hawksmoor and Henry Keene 1720–91

Worcester College, Sainsbury Building

The Sainsbury Building, housing new student rooms, was a result of an endowment to the college from the Sainsbury family, of supermarket fame. The architects selected for the commission were the London firm MacCormac Jamieson and Prichard, this being their first building in Oxford.

The new building is sited away from the main college buildings, at the end of a picturesque lake. It is L-shaped in plan, formally conceived about the diagonal axis, which is particularly apparent from the lake-side view of the building. The main entrance, the entrance to the staircases in each of the wings, and the major communal rooms on the ground floor are grouped symmetrically about this diagonal, and it could be argued that the diagonal emphasis results in a slightly congested plan.

Despite the strict geometry of the plan, the building form is picturesque, appearing as a series of stacked blocks rising to four storeys in the middle. Each block represents a room and is given a separate identity with its own split-pedimented roof and timber bay window. Terraces afford pleasant views of the gardens. The dominant materials – buff brickwork, stone, slate and timber – are of good quality, and the detailing is handled with care and fluency, although the theme of repeated squares internally is a little over-insistent. There is also a delightful small gate lodge at the end of Worcester Place, which has a witty split-pedimented roof.

This building marked a transition from the international college architecture of the 1970s to a more relaxed, picturesque architecture inspired by the small-scale domestic architecture of Oxford.

ADDRESS Worcester Street
ACCESS college open daily: term 14.00–18.00; vacation 09.00–12.00, 14.00–18.00; visible from Worcester Place

MacCormac Jamieson and Prichard 1982

MacCormac Jamieson and Prichard 1982

Worcester College, Linbury Building

A decade after the completion of the Sainsbury Building (page 198), Worcester College commissioned a second building to provide further student accommodation and meeting rooms. The architects selected were Maguire and Murray who, like MacCormac Jamieson and Prichard, had a good track record of Oxbridge college work (pages 192 and 304).

The Linbury Building is located on the southern boundary of the college, adjacent to Hythe Bridge Street. The building sits behind an existing high stone boundary wall and takes the form of a series of linked square towers which step up towards the corner of Hythe Bridge Street and Worcester Street. The accommodation is planned in the traditional Oxford manner, with study-bedrooms arranged off communal staircases. In this case each tower represents a stack of rooms. The towers have a defensive imagery expressed by the use of small, irregularly placed window openings punched into the otherwise blank, stone-coloured, roughcast walls. A certain delicacy is provided by the lifted pyramidal roofs that appear to float above each tower.

The college side of the scheme is less severe and the towers appear to cascade away from the existing college buildings, finishing in a single-storey meeting room, which has a lead-covered pyramidal roof form detailed to give it a delicate Japanese imagery.

ADDRESS Worcester Street
ACCESS college open daily: term 14.00–18.00; vacation 09.00–12.00, 14.00–18.00; visible from Hythe Bridge Street

Maguire and Murray 1991

Maguire and Murray 1991

Colleges: north-east of St Mary's

All Souls College, Front Quadrangle

All Souls College was founded in 1438 by Henry Chichele, Archbishop of Canterbury, as an ecclesiastical community. He had graduated from New College, which provided the architectural model for All Souls. The master mason and designer was Richard Chevynton, All Souls being his only recorded work. The first buildings were grouped around Front Quadrangle and entered via a four-storey gate tower from High Street.

The style is Perpendicular gothic, in which rectilinear forms predominate. The gate tower entrance archway has fine gothic lierne vaulting in two bays. The east, south and west ranges are two-storeyed, and designed as residential accommodation of shared chambers with studies partitioned off in the corners. The elevations have square-headed windows and doorways, and embattled parapets on both façades. The High Street and Catte Street elevations were ruthlessly regothicised by Daniel Robertson (1826–27), of Oxford University Press fame (page 114). The library, originally of eight bays on the upper floor of the east range, was moved to the Codrington Library in the eighteenth century (page 208).

The chapel is on the north side of the quadrangle facing the entrance. The medieval hall is attached to the east end of the chapel and was rebuilt by Hawksmoor in 1730–33 in a matching style. While the chapel is smaller than that at New College, it has the same T-shaped plan and ornamentation. The hammerbeam roof, tiers of saints carved on the stone reredos (restored by Sir George Gilbert Scott in 1870–79), carved wooden stalls with their misericords, and stained glass in the eastern windows of the antechapel are original. The classical screen is eighteenth century.

ADDRESS High Street
ACCESS college open Monday–Friday 14.00–16.30 (4 November–end February 14.00–16.00)

Richard Chevynton (master mason) 1438–43

Colleges: north-east of St Mary's

Richard Chevynton (master mason) 1438–43

All Souls College, Warden's Lodging

In the early eighteenth century All Souls went through a period of expansion, and the existing accommodation became increasingly inadequate. In 1703 Dr George Clarke, then Warden, offered to finance the building of a new Warden's lodging. Clarke tried his hand at architecture, often in collaboration with others, and was involved in almost every early eighteenth-century college and university building in Oxford.

The new lodging was originally to be sited on vacant land to the north of the college, adjacent to Hertford College, but Clarke located it instead on the High Street frontage to the east of Front Quadrangle. Building began in 1704. The original design, attributed to Clarke, was in a plain classical style, but what is seen today is the result of a refacing in the Palladian style by Daniel Robertson in 1825, who also designed Oxford University Press (1826–28) on Walton Street (page 114).

The house has a simple rectangular plan, two rooms deep and two wide, with a staircase centrally placed towards the front of the plan. It is two storeys high, with attics and cellars, and has an ashlar façade to High Street of six regular bays with a rusticated lower storey. The end bays project slightly, and the upper windows are given emphasis with applied square hoods supported on brackets. Robertson's refacing removed the original embattled parapet, and relocated the front door from the eastern-most bay of the High Street elevation to its present central position. The Warden's lodgings demonstrate a new eighteenth-century attitude to the world outside by presenting the primary façade and main entrance to the street rather than to the college.

ADDRESS High Street
ACCESS none; visible from High Street

Dr George Clarke 1703–06, Daniel Robertson 1827–29

Dr George Clarke 1703–06, Daniel Robertson 1827–29

All Souls College, North Quadrangle, Codrington Library and Hall

In the early eighteenth century Dr George Clarke, then Warden, proposed a plan for the expansion of the college with a new quadrangle to the north, on the site of the medieval cloister. He invited prominent architects to work up his designs, and Nicholas Hawksmoor was selected to carry out the work. The final design had a new quadrangle, with a library on the north (1716–40), fellows' sets on the east, a new hall in line with the existing chapel on the south (1730–33), and a colonnade screening the quadrangle from Radcliffe Square to the west. Hawksmoor designed the new buildings in his version of gothic, following the style of the chapel.

Hawksmoor's sense of urban design led to an alignment of the quadrangle with the newly created Radcliffe Square, rather than with Front Quadrangle (page 204), closing the new east–west axis with central twin towers topped by slender pinnacled turrets, flanking the common room. The cloister screen to Radcliffe Square (1728–34), with central gateway and cupola, is in what Hawksmoor called 'the Monastik manner'.

The plan and elevations of the new library followed those of the medieval chapel. Inside, the design deviates from Hawksmoor's intentions: it was fitted out in a Palladian manner by James Gibbs after Hawksmoor's death in 1736. The spectacular single volume is lined with two-storey, painted-timber bookshelves set in bays formed by Ionic pilasters.

The exterior of the new hall also followed the pattern of the existing chapel, but inside Hawksmoor's originality found expression. The coffered ceiling with its apsidal ends is of particular note.

ADDRESS High Street
ACCESS college open Monday–Friday 14.00–16.30 (4 November–end February 14.00–16.00)

Nicholas Hawksmoor 1716–36

Colleges: north-east of St Mary's

Nicholas Hawksmoor 1716–36

Balliol College, Martin Building

The Martin Building was designed as a graduates' centre for both Balliol and St Anne's Colleges. The pavilion-like building sits back from St Cross Road and faces the Law, English, Economics & Statistics Libraries (page 128), also by Sir Leslie Martin. A second phase was originally planned, which would have doubled the accommodation, but only the first phase was built. The two buildings are clearly from the same architectural fold, although the Martin Building, with its solid, defensive brick form pierced by small openings, has greater affinity with Martin's Harvey Court, Cambridge.

The front façade is carefully composed, with slot windows and a projecting timber-clad staircase enclosure, again like Harvey Court, but it fails to signal the position of its entrance. Strangely the building offers no clue to its use, and is often thought to be a sports pavilion.

The internal accommodation faces Balliol Sports Ground. Here the elevation is treated in a more open manner, consisting of three storeys of bands of brickwork alternating with broad bands of strip windows.

ADDRESS St Cross Road, opposite the Law, English, Economics & Statistics Libraries
ACCESS none; visible from St Cross Road and Mansfield Road

Sir Leslie Martin with David Owers 1968–69

Sir Leslie Martin with David Owers 1968–69

Balliol College, Jowett Building

With few open development sites left in central Oxford, Balliol College has resorted to building on the edges of its playing fields. MacCormac Jamieson and Prichard have planned a vast new complex of student residences on the southern edge of Balliol's cricket ground, of which the Jowett Building is the first phase.

The external massing of the complex, towers grouped in an accretive and picturesque manner, is reminiscent of a medieval fortress or an Italian hill town. The towers, with groups of student rooms accessed off communal staircases, are arranged to form small linked quadrangles with open aspects to the cricket ground to the north and to Jowett Walk to the south. The towers are cut into from roof level by large metal and glass projecting bay windows rising through two or three storeys, beneath which are small punched window openings at ground-floor level. The effect is of children's building blocks with huge castellations, and appears to abandon the practice's customary meticulous articulation of the smaller elements of building (pages 180, 198 and 262). The external walls are of buff Oxford stock brick banded at regular intervals with single courses of blue engineering brick, perhaps alluding to rustication or to the polychromy of William Butterfield's High Victorian gothic Keble College (page 156).

ADDRESS Jowett Walk
ACCESS none; visible from Jowett Walk

MacCormac Jamieson and Prichard 1996

Colleges: north-east of St Mary's

MacCormac Jamieson and Prichard 1996

Hertford College, Old Buildings Quadrangle

In 1820–22, when the site was owned by Magdalen Hall, William Garbett had designed a pair of Palladian blocks, one each side of the seventeenth-century gate tower. In 1874 Hertford College was refounded, and in 1887–79, after the gate tower had been pulled down to widen Catte Street, Sir Thomas G Jackson built the central block, linking Garbett's flanking wings. Jackson's eclectic classical composition is framed by two bays and has a central entrance, above which are three Venetian windows separated by Corinthian columns. The college dining hall is on the first floor, with the high table behind the upper two windows of the right hand bay. Jackson sought historical continuity: the frieze of drinking harts, the college's device, is a pun on Hart Hall, which occupied the site from 1282, while the late seventeenth-century wooden gate from the demolished gate tower was reused.

Inside the quadrangle is the spiral staircase leading to the hall, modelled on a French Renaissance precedent at Blois, but given Jacobean details. The block to its right, as the Venetian windows suggest, was also designed by Jackson, in 1890.

To the south is Jackson's chapel of 1908. The octagonal tower, surmounted by eight, free-standing columns and a dome, is a counter-point to the Blois stair tower across the quadrangle. Alongside, the old chapel of 1716 is now a library, while diagonally opposite, the Elizabethan old hall of Hart Hall is the oldest surviving part of the original buildings, which also extend along the eastern side of the quadrangle.

ADDRESS Catte Street
ACCESS college open daily 10.00–dusk

Sir Thomas G Jackson 1887–1908

Colleges: north-east of St Mary's

Sir Thomas G Jackson 1887–1908

Hertford College, Bridge of Sighs and North Quadrangle

When Hertford College decided to expand to the north across New College Lane, on to a site of old houses owned by the city, it again employed Sir Thomas G Jackson, whose work at Old Buildings Quadrangle (page 214) had been so successful.

Jackson proposed a bridge across the lane to connect the two parts of the college, and produced a design based on the *Ponte dei Sospiri* in Venice (designed by Antonio Contino and built *c.*1600) that connects the Doges' Palace with the prison across the canal. The Venetian model had also been used as inspiration in 1831 by Henry Hutchinson at St John's College, Cambridge. Jackson's bridge is now a popular landmark.

With North Quadrangle, Jackson reverted for inspiration to England in the seventeenth century, using his familiar amalgam of Tudor gables, canted bay windows, cross windows, and attached columns. A small octagonal chapel of about 1520, with an attractive south doorway and carved lintel, was also incorporated. This was originally known as the Chapel of Our Lady at Smith Gate, and was built on a bastion of the original city wall beside an entrance gate. The pyramidal roof and intermediate floor were added by Jackson in 1931.

ADDRESS bridge: New College Lane; chapel: Catte Street
ACCESS college open daily 10.00–dusk; bridge visible from New College Lane

Sir Thomas G Jackson 1913–14

Sir Thomas G Jackson 1913–14

Lady Margaret Hall, Wolfson Quadrangle

Lady Margaret Hall, named after the mother of Henry VII, was founded in 1878 and was the first women's college in Oxford. Old Hall, a house at the end of Norham Gardens, was its first home, and was extended in 1881–84 in a red brick Queen Anne style by Sir Basil Champneys.

The entrance to the college is now through a fine pedimented stone gateway in the centre of a dignified red brick neo-Georgian range designed in 1957–61 by Raymond Erith. By reducing the windows to a minimum, he wished to imbue the range with 'simplicity and repose', an effect also achieved in his 1958–60 Provost's lodgings for The Queen's College, New College Lane. The dry moat in front of the college was a device to accommodate a change in ground level, and was meant to be part of a larger forecourt. Inside Wolfson Quadrangle, the red brick library range on the left is also by Erith. The ground-floor bookstack is articulated by structural monolithic stone piers; the two upper levels have windows lighting individual desks between bookcases, while the lunettes give general illumination above the gallery level.

Opposite the entrance to the quadrangle is the Talbot Building of 1909, designed by Sir Reginald Blomfield. He designed the college's first expansion, a series of linked pavilions in a uniform William and Mary style, reminiscent of that at Hampton Court. These are best seen from the garden. Talbot Building was at one time the college's entrance, and contained the hall with the library above. Lodge Building, which forms the south side of the quadrangle, was built by Blomfield in 1926 and connects his earlier pavilions with Old Hall.

ADDRESS Norham Gardens, north end
ACCESS apply to porter's lodge

Sir Reginald Blomfield 1896–1926, Raymond Erith 1957–61

Sir Reginald Blomfield 1896–1926, Raymond Erith 1957–61

Lady Margaret Hall, Deneke Building and Chapel

With the construction of the Deneke Building in 1931, Lady Margaret Hall doubled its size, and relocated its dining hall from Sir Reginald Blomfield's Talbot Building (page 218).

Sir Giles Gilbert Scott, grandson of Sir George, had successfully used a similar greyish brick with Adamesque stone dressings and Georgian windows in 1924, for his Memorial Court at Clare College, Cambridge. At Deneke Building the effect is less happy. This vast, relentlessly symmetrical, three-storey elongated block, with its stretched central pediment, seems to bear no relationship either to collegiate tradition, as at Clare, or to Blomfield's red brick pavilions. Nor can it be said to enhance Lady Margaret Hall's attractive water meadow location.

The chapel of the same date is Byzantine in style, and has a Greek cross plan. Originally connected to Deneke Building and the rest of the college by two open colonnades (now clumsily infilled), it is equally difficult to place in any local tradition, although its massive walls and simple forms are architecturally more satisfying.

ADDRESS Norham Gardens, north end
ACCESS apply to porter's lodge

Sir Giles Gilbert Scott 1931, 1932

Sir Giles Gilbert Scott 1931, 1932

Linacre College, Abraham Building

In 1978 Linacre College, a small college for graduates, moved from the premises of the St Catherine's Society in St Aldate's to the present site. In 1994 Energy Conscious Design was commissioned to design a new 'green' residential building for the college. On the insistence of the planners the new building had to follow the style of the existing Queen Anne style buildings; tall, four-storey, red brick blocks with regularly spaced, white-painted sash windows and Dutch gables.

The Abraham Building, an L-shaped range located on the southern boundary of the site, looks almost identical to its predecessors, yet it is an extremely low-energy building, both in terms of the use of 'embodied energy' – that is the energy consumed in the production of the materials used – and in terms of the energy the building uses daily. The energy-efficient features include highly insulated walls, the recycling of waste water from baths, basins and gutters, and the planting of 16 hectares of Tasmanian eucalyptus forest, intended to offset the carbon monoxide emissions produced by the gas and electricity used by the building.

Despite the architects' attempt to mimic the original buildings, the detailing is less ornate and the quality of construction less elegant, resulting in a rather disappointing exterior.

ADDRESS St Cross Road
ACCESS college open daily 09.00–17.00

Energy Conscious Design 1994

Energy Conscious Design 1994

Magdalen College, Great Quadrangle and Chapel

In 1458 William of Waynflete, Bishop of Winchester and Lord Chancellor, acquired the old Hospital of St John between the East Gate and the river as the site for his new college, and between 1467 and 1474 erected the boundary wall, which now encloses the deer park.

Work on the buildings took place from 1475 to 1490. Consisting of chapel, hall, cloister, library, Muniment Tower and Founder's Tower the whole ensemble is a fine example of a late fifteenth-century college plan, and is attributable to William Orchard. As at New College (page 234), the antechapel and chapel are T-shaped in plan. The hall is continuous with the chapel at first-floor level, and forms a grand south elevation to the Great Quadrangle, complete with buttresses and pinnacles.

The quadrangle is surrounded by a cloister, and entry to both chapel and cloister is beneath the Muniment Tower, built to contain the college archives. The Founder's Tower of 1479 originally housed the President's lodgings, and provides the formal entry to the college. The bay window was added to the hall in the late seventeenth century. The chapel was re-roofed in 1790–96 by James Wyatt, and in 1829–34 it was thoroughly restored in an appropriately gothic style by Lewis N Cottingham.

The cloister, built with a second storey covering the walkway on three sides, had a third storey of tall dormer windows added in the sixteenth century. The north range was rebuilt in 1824 to a more uniform design, including the removal of the dormers, and much of the east side was rebuilt in 1825–27. The heraldic supporters on the buttresses are nineteenth-century copies of early sixteenth-century originals.

ADDRESS High Street, east end
ACCESS college open daily 14.00–18.00

William Orchard (master mason) 1475–90

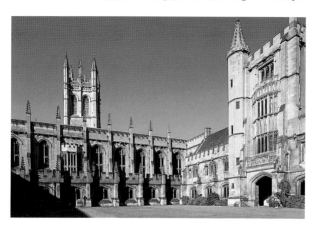

Colleges: north-east of St Mary's

William Orchard (master mason) 1475–90

Magdalen College, Bell Tower

After the completion of Magdalen College in 1490 (page 224), a subscription was raised to build a new bell tower. This was possibly intended to be a replacement for a belfry remaining from the old Hospital of St John, whose thirteenth-century chapel is incorporated into the range of buildings to the west of the tower (marked by an external pulpit in the corner of St John's Quadrangle), which may explain why the range is aligned with the street and not the chapel.

The tower is a fine example of Perpendicular gothic work, though rather plain and late compared with the notable Perpendicular gothic towers of some of the local Cotswold wool churches, for example at Chipping Campden. The similar tower over the crossing at Merton College Chapel (page 292) had also been completed nearly 40 years before Magdalen was started. That having been said, the ornate top storey with its eight crocketed pinnacles, fretwork balustrade, octagonal corner buttresses and deeply recessed bell openings is most attractive, and the sheer height of the tower makes it a fine landmark for visitors entering the city across Magdalen Bridge.

The tower was intended to be free-standing, but was soon abutted by the buildings that now enclose Chaplain's Yard.

ADDRESS High Street, east end
ACCESS none; visible from High Street

William Raynold (master mason) 1492–1509

William Raynold (master mason) 1492–1509

Magdalen College, New Buildings

From the 1720s Magdalen College was concerned about the state of its medieval buildings. In 1728 Edward Holdsworth, a fellow of the college, prepared a plan for a major redevelopment and extension, which was adopted after consultation with James Gibbs, among others. Holdsworth envisaged the demolition of much of the medieval cloister, and the construction to the north of a vast new classical quadrangle incorporating a loggia, linked to the medieval chapel and hall by two short arms of the remaining part of the cloister. On the west side of the new quadrangle would be a magnificent library, and in front of that an oval forecourt with railings and gates facing Longwall Street, flanked by pavilions containing new lodgings for the President and the Lecturer in Theology. Despite revisions being proposed by Nicholas Hawksmoor in 1734, only the north range of this ambitious project – now known as New Buildings – was built, complete with loggia and five pedimented central bays. Although an impressive building in its own right, its unfinished return ends remained a constant reminder of Holdsworth's incomplete scheme.

In 1791 James Wyatt proposed giving the building a gothic face and linking it to the cloister. In 1801 John Nash and Humphry Repton also produced gothic schemes for completing the quadrangle, both of which also addressed the problem of landscaping the Deer Park, Repton proposing a lake. From 1822 Thomas Harrison made similar proposals, both classical and gothic. In the end the college decided to ask him, in 1824, to finish off the ends of the building with uniform, forward-stepping bays, a modest conclusion to an ambitious plan.

ADDRESS High Street, north side
ACCESS college open daily 14.00–18.00

Edward Holdsworth 1733–34, Thomas Harrison 1824

Edward Holdsworth 1733–34, Thomas Harrison 1824

Magdalen College, Grove Buildings

Demetri Porphyrios' winning entry to a limited competition for a new range of buildings, the Grove Buildings, demonstrated his interest in the accretive morphology of the Oxford colleges. The site for the new buildings was on the western edge of the Deer Park, sitting behind the high medieval wall which encloses the college grounds. The brief included a theatre, communal rooms, and student rooms, these last to be arranged in the traditional Oxford manner of sets of two or four rooms per landing off a communal stair. Porphyrios' design fragments the accommodation into five separate blocks, and groups these in a relaxed, almost picturesque, manner around a trapezoidal garden court. The court is raised on a terrace overlooking the Deer Park. Each block is given a form loosely based on its typological precedent: a pavilion-like form for the theatre, and linear ranges for the student accommodation.

The architectural language is eclectic. A different architectural style is selected for each building, and is drawn from works in the surrounding context. Thus the residential Arcade Building takes its cue from the adjacent Longwall Quadrangle of 1932 by Sir Giles Gilbert Scott, which interestingly was also built as a revival of the gothic style. The gable-ended Theatre Building is designed in a classical style, taking its cue from Magdalen New Buildings (page 228) beyond it to the east. Despite this heterogeneous approach, the repeated use of castellations, towers, solid ashlar construction with small stone-mullioned windows, and steeply pitched stone tile roofs with dormers and chimneys gives the scheme an overall air of picturesque gothic.

ADDRESS High Street
ACCESS college open daily 14.00–18.00; partly visible from Longwall Street

Demetri Porphyrios 1995

Colleges: north-east of St Mary's

Demetri Porphyrios 1995

Mansfield College

Mansfield College bears the name of the family that in 1838 founded Spring Hill College in Birmingham, a congregationalist theological college. In 1886, following the relaxation of the university's attitude to Nonconformism, the college was refounded in Oxford.

The Hampstead architect Basil Champneys had previously worked in both Cambridge and Oxford, producing red brick buildings with white-painted windows in the Queen Anne style for the newly founded womens' colleges of Newnham and Lady Margaret Hall. For Mansfield Champneys instead chose stone and the gothic style, producing his best set of buildings in Oxford.

Rejecting the traditional closed quadrangular college layout, Champneys implied enclosure by placing buildings on three sides of a central green space. With lyrical ease he assembled a south-facing range composed of a selection of fifteenth-century Oxford collegiate motifs: a gate tower with an oriel window, to its right a hall with an ample bay window, and a two-storey library to the left, whose barn-like galleried timber interior has a fine painted timber roof. The chapel, on the east side, has an altar that, unconventionally, faces north. The entrance to the college is from Mansfield Road, and not through the gate tower as might be expected. The block to the south was designed by Thomas Rayson in 1962.

ADDRESS Mansfield Road
ACCESS open daily 09.00–17.00

Basil Champneys 1887–89

Basil Champneys 1887–89

New College, Great Quadrangle and Chapel

William of Wykeham, Bishop of Winchester and Lord Chancellor, used the master mason William Wynford to build his large new college on wasteland just inside the north walls of the city. Construction took place from 1380 to 1386, with the cloister and barn continuing till 1402.

The Great Quadrangle is entered under a three-storey gate tower, the first in Oxford, built to house the warden's lodging. The tall chapel and hall were built end to end along the north side, just inside the city wall, with the antechapel projecting into one corner. This mirrors the Muniment Tower in the north-east corner, where a vaulted staircase leads to the first-floor hall. The quadrangle, originally of two storeys, has residential accommodation, the first case where both fellows and students lodged in the same college. An assortment of attic dormers was rebuilt as a third storey in 1634, and the windows enlarged with sashes in 1718. In 1386 the kitchen extended the hall eastwards, while alongside Queen's Lane, a communal latrine of two storeys, the Long Room, was also built.

The huge chapel had the first T-shaped plan in Oxford, but the cloister (page 236) stopped any extension of the short nave. The Perpendicular gothic windows are original, but the glass is eighteenth century. In 1877–81 Sir George Gilbert Scott rebuilt the hammerbeam roof and James Wyatt's 1789–94 reredos on the east wall, also designing the stalls reusing the medieval misericords. His earlier tied roof replacement for the hall is better, and complements the linenfold panelling and screen of 1533–55.

ADDRESS New College Lane
ACCESS college open: term Monday–Friday 14.00–17.00, Saturday–Sunday 11.00–17.00; vacation 11.00–17.00; admission charge

William Wynford (master mason) 1380–86

William Wynford (master mason) 1380–86

New College, Cloister and Bell Tower

The narrow approach to the gate tower of New College down New College Lane is flanked by two austere, almost windowless, medieval walls of approximately equal height. To the right is the rear wall of the Warden's Barn, erected in 1402 for the storage of hay and stabling. In 1676 the barn was linked by a bridge to the Warden's lodgings, and converted so that it could also house guests. To the left stands the cloister.

New College Lane took its present form when it was re-routed around the site of the cloister, which was enclosed as a graveyard and dedicated in 1400. Entered from the Great Quadrangle beside the antechapel, the cloister extends to the west the linear sequence of kitchen, hall, chapel and antechapel, and uses the city wall defensively as its north wall. Its Perpendicular gothic tracery, buttresses, and painted timber roof are all contemporary with the chapel, whose west wall rises behind as a magnificent backdrop.

The bell tower, built in 1400 and first fitted with a clock in 1455, became one of the bastions in the city wall, and no doubt also functioned as a look-out. The ensemble of chapel, bell tower and cloister, with its asymmetrically placed holm-oak, is one of Oxford's most delightful and tranquil places.

ADDRESS New College Lane
ACCESS college open: term Monday–Friday 14.00–17.00, Saturday–Sunday 11.00–17.00; vacation 11.00–17.00; admission charge

1386–1400

1386–1400

New College, Garden Quadrangle

The garden, reached from the Great Quadrangle via a gateway under the library, was first a kitchen garden, and was laid out formally only in 1530. Protected from north and east winds by a long stretch of the city walls of 1226–40, it is dominated by a central formal mount. This was started in 1549, made larger in 1616 and 1623, and given stone steps and a look-out seat in 1649. The mount's wilderness appearance dates from 1762.

A treasury projecting into the garden had been built on to the north side of the garden gateway in 1440, and a second-floor library added some 40 years later. When extending the college into the garden in 1682, William Byrd, master mason, first considered a closed quadrangle, but eventually opted for an open version stepping back like Sir Christopher Wren's contemporary plan for Winchester Palace, which had in turn been influenced by the palace of Versailles. He therefore repeated the treasury block to the south, before building two parallel three-storey residential wings projecting into the garden. These successfully masked the kitchen and latrine, or Long Room (page 234). Built of ashlar, they were given alternating segmental and triangular pediments over the windows, and battlemented parapets. Byrd's scheme was completed with end pavilions in a similar style to the south in 1700, and to the north in 1707, and enclosed by iron railings and a gate in 1711.

Remodelling began in 1718, when Byrd's stone mullions and transoms, along with the gothic windows in the Great Quadrangle, were replaced with sash windows, giving an elegant Georgian appearance.

ADDRESS New College Lane
ACCESS college open: term Monday–Friday 14.00–17.00, Saturday–Sunday 11.00–17.00; vacation 11.00–17.00; admission charge

William Byrd (master mason) 1682–83 and eighteenth century

William Byrd (master mason) 1682–83 and eighteenth century

New College, Sacher Building

David Roberts' practice was in Cambridge, where he also lectured at the School of Architecture. Meanwhile he produced a series of modest buildings for the Cambridge colleges, starting in 1954 with Mallory Court for Magdalene, his own college.

The three-storey Sacher Building at New college, named after college benefactors, provides accommodation for graduate students. It is accessed across the college garden, through a newly created opening in the medieval city wall, which faces the building across a small courtyard. Here, the modern elevation of strip windows and exposed beam ends, so characteristic of its time, is given a central emphasis, with a recessed terrace on the top floor looking back over the wall, and full-height glazing to a common room at ground level. The end bays are also recessed. The front on to Longwall Street has a plainer treatment, with a protective wall at street level.

The building has recently become a *bête noire* for the detractors of modern architecture. Although of the same height, it is criticised for its failure to relate obviously to the adjacent vernacular houses, in a way that Oxford's Georgian architecture, so new in its time, never was. Ironically, Magdalen College's Grove Buildings (page 230), which so clearly represent the present-day loss of nerve, face it across Longwall Street. It is hoped that Roberts' serious contribution to the architecture of his day survives its present-day reviling.

ADDRESS Longwall Street, and via New College garden
ACCESS college open: term Monday–Friday 14.00–17.00, Saturday–Sunday 11.00–17.00; vacation 11.00–17.00; admission charge

David Roberts 1961–62

David Roberts 1961–62

The Queen's College, North Quadrangle

Work in The Queen's College North Quadrangle was to initiate the most ambitious rebuilding of an entire medieval Oxford college. In 1672, Sir Christopher Wren provided a design for a new residential block to be built in the gardens to the north of the original medieval quadrangle. What remains of Wren's Williamson Building can only be seen from Queen's Lane. Where the lane turns left, the end of the block, with cross-shaped windows flanking alcoves, is Wren's original design. The remainder of the block, opposite St Peter-in-the-East, has later sash windows. Wren became Surveyor of the King's Works in 1669, and by 1672 was busy rebuilding London after the great fire, so he may not have given much time to this design.

The library (page 244), built in the garden east of Wren's building, followed in 1692–95. In 1707 the North Quadrangle's north range was built between the library and Wren's building. It is a plain classical range of three storeys, probably designed by the college master mason, John Townesend. The balustrade, added to mask an attic storey, is later.

By 1710 Dr George Clarke had devised a coherent plan for the whole college. Redevelopment of the medieval Front Quadrangle (page 246) started with the hall and chapel, and was completed in 1719 with William Townesend, John's son, as master mason. The south range of North Quadrangle, including the kitchen, was then built in 1719 to match the north range, to the rear of the newly completed hall and chapel. The matching east range followed in 1719, completing the quadrangle. This meant building on to the front of Wren's block at an angle, hiding it entirely from view from the quadrangle.

ADDRESS High Street, north side
ACCESS apply to domestic bursar

Sir Christopher Wren 1672, John and William Townesend 1707–19

Sir Christopher Wren 1672, John and William Townesend 1707–19

The Queen's College, Library

Henry Aldrich became Dean of Christ Church in 1689 and Vice-Chancellor of the university in 1692. He was a man of great learning, and a gifted architectural expert who was consulted on most college projects at this time. There is a drawing of his dated 1693 of a building sufficiently like The Queen's College library for the attribution to be made. The master mason was John Townesend.

Sir Christopher Wren's free-standing classical library of 1671–78 for Trinity College, Cambridge, provided the model: a first-floor hall with round-arched windows, above an open arcade. The Trinity arcade, provided because of the risk of flooding, has remained open, while that at Queen's, less justified functionally, was enclosed by Charles R Cockerell in 1841 to provide further accommodation for the library. Although the entrance and stairs are at the south end, Aldrich gave his imposing building a strong central emphasis, using a pediment, pilasters and carved enrichment, an approach rejected by Wren at Trinity in favour of a more subtle modelling. The west façade, facing the Provost's garden, is even more heavily enriched.

The inside is superb, with finely carved bookcases, alternating with reading desks, projecting into the room between the windows, leaving a central passageway. At Trinity, Wren's skilful section allowed the bookcases to be below the windows: here they are at the same level. There is a particularly fine stucco ceiling of 1695 by James Hands, whose panels were given rococo decoration by Thomas Roberts in 1756.

ADDRESS High Street, north side
ACCESS apply to domestic bursar

Dean Henry Aldrich 1692–95

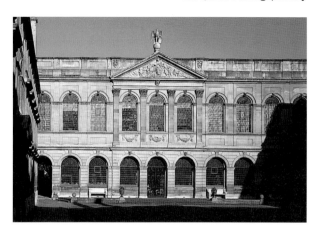

Dean Henry Aldrich 1692–95

The Queen's College, Front Quadrangle

Dr George Clarke, Fellow of All Souls College, became Oxford's foremost architectural expert when Dean Henry Aldrich died in 1710. The Queen's College was committed to the redevelopment of its medieval quadrangle to a classical plan evolved by Clarke, which was more manageable than the schemes submitted by Nicholas Hawksmoor. William Townesend was master mason, and probably helped develop the designs of the buildings.

Clarke's final scheme placed the hall and chapel (1714–19) opposite the gateway, as at University College (page 310), built some 75 years earlier. Here, however, they form a grand unified pedimented classical composition, with a projecting central bay and a tall baroque cupola. This arrangement had been used in 1682–89 by Sir Christopher Wren at the Chelsea Hospital, London, and the giant order was similar to Hawksmoor's at The Clarendon Building (page 110). Hawksmoor may have commented on the design, and the fine interiors, particularly of the hall, perhaps owe something to him.

The austerely detailed colonnaded residential blocks to the west (1710) and the east (1735–60) form a south-facing open quadrangle screened from the street in the manner of a Parisian town house. French in spirit too are the central attics crowned by a segmental pediment. Hawksmoor is credited with the rusticated screen and entrance of 1734, which creates one of Oxford's most memorable street frontages, while continuing the colonnade within the quadrangle. Above the gateway an elegant circular temple houses a statue by Henry Cheere, of Caroline, queen of George II, who was a patron and benefactor of the college.

ADDRESS High Street, north side
ACCESS apply to domestic bursar

Dr G Clarke with W Townesend 1710–60, N Hawksmoor 1734

Colleges: north-east of St Mary's

Dr G Clarke with W Townesend 1710–60, N Hawksmoor 1734

The Queen's College, Florey Building

The Florey building was the last in the triumvirate of extraordinary constructivist-inspired buildings James Stirling designed in the 1960s, the others being Leicester University Engineering Building (1959–63) and the History Faculty Building, Cambridge (1964–68).

When Stirling was commissioned to design new student rooms for Queen's he used the Oxford quadrangle tradition as the generator for the form. Four storeys of students' rooms wrap around three sides of a quadrangle, which looks towards Magdalen Bell Tower (page 226). The building has a cranked U-shaped form propped one storey off the ground on a splay-legged, concrete A-frame, forming a covered cloister-like walkway at ground-floor level. The external elevations rake out, and read as solid planes of red tile, with small horizontal slot openings which light the corridors and service spaces. The inside of the U-shape has a fully glazed façade which steps back, with the student rooms behind. The top-floor rooms are spatially exciting, and are double height with mezzanines. Circulation and service areas are wrapped around the outside of the plan, but vertical circulation is via a detached staircase tower, located by the entrance. Communal facilities are located under the grassed central courtyard, and are lit by clerestory windows to the north.

The building can easily be criticised: its strong form sits awkwardly in its urban context, the entrance is hard to find, the student rooms have poor environmental control and lack privacy, and the building has weathered poorly. Nevertheless, this uncompromising essay in neo-constructivist expressionism helped to shake the British architectural scene out of its cosy post-war complacency, and as such is important.

ADDRESS St Clement's Street
ACCESS none; visible from St Clement's Street

James Stirling and Partners 1966–71

James Stirling and Partners 1966–71

St Catherine's College

St Catherine's College is a masterpiece of conceptual thought, designed, right down to the table cutlery, by Arne Jacobsen. It leaves nothing to accident, and in its abstract thoroughness is most un-English.

The elements of the composition are disposed on a level paved platform: two parallel, linear residential blocks facing east and west, between which are placed the communal parts of the college in a third, discontinuous, line. The unhierarchical geometry appears to be anti-monumental and egalitarian. The language of structure and materials is subjected to a discipline of separation: the concrete frame is always expressed, and walls (which are of a purpose-made buff-coloured two-inch brick inside and out), are treated as infill panels. Glazing, using bronze frames in the communal buildings and black-finished aluminium elsewhere, either fills an entire wall or is used to separate infill from structure. Certain elements act as a counterpoint to the planning grid: an octagonal music room, a circular bicycle shelter, a concrete bell tower, a Barbara Hepworth sculpture and carefully placed trees. The site is beautifully landscaped, using fin-like screen walls to articulate the spaces, and the entrance – originally intended to be realigned from the river Cherwell – is across a formal canal and water garden.

Yet, for all its 'Scandinavian' modernism, there are Oxford references. With the exception of a chapel, catered for by St Cross church (page 82) nearby, the distinct elements of a college are all present: students' rooms are arranged on staircases, not corridors; most buildings have cloister-like, covered walkways; and quadrangles are implied by the placing of the buildings.

ADDRESS Manor Road, south end
ACCESS gardens open daily 14.00–17.00

Arne Jacobsen 1960–64

Colleges: north-east of St Mary's

Arne Jacobsen 1960–64

St Catherine's College, New Student Rooms

St Catherine's College remained unaltered from Arne Jacobsen's original plan (page 250) until Hodder Associates designed 55 new student residences on a site opposite the entrance. The new design is respectful, but not slavish, in its response to the powerful geometry and ruthlessly consistent minimalist language of Jacobsen's college.

The design groups the new accommodation into three two-storey blocks, with staircases running in glazed links between them. The first glimpse of the building is of the southernmost glass staircase, which has a skilful, De Stijl-like, minimal design. Each two-storey residential unit contains eight *en suite* student rooms on each floor, which are accessed from a short double-sided corridor, with a staircase at one end and pantry at the other. The blocks are raised on a one-storey brick podium, which contains communal rooms and stores. They have precast concrete façades intended to allude to the vertical rhythm of Jacobsen's elevations. The residential units are staggered along their length to follow the line of the stream to the rear, while the podium is aligned with the rest of the college, providing a ground-level walkway under the cantilevered blocks. This geometrical shift gives a curious, slightly contrived effect, largely because the alignment of the stream is given dominance over the geometry of the college. The elevation to the rear is more simple and omits the cantilever at first floor-level.

At present the scheme suffers from having a car parking area at the front. It is intended that a second block be built on the east side of the car park, which will then become a new pedestrian quadrangle.

ADDRESS Manor Road
ACCESS none; visible from college entrance at the end of Manor Road

Hodder Associates 1995

Hodder Associates 1995

St Edmund Hall, Front Quadrangle

St Edmund Hall is named after St Edmund of Abington, Archbishop of Canterbury in 1234–40, and may be built on the site of the house where he once lived. As an academic hall, mentioned as early as 1317, it has neither founder nor statutes, and became a college only in 1957.

None of the medieval buildings remain, although Front Quadrangle has a medieval flavour and is one of the most intimate and attractive college spaces in Oxford. The west end of the north range was built between 1581 and 1600, and in 1601–09 the small house to the right of the present chapel was added. The main entrance to the college from Queen's Lane is through a small passage in a part of the building constructed about 1635, which includes the President's lodging, marked by an oriel window. The hall to its north was built in 1659, and still looks medieval with its tall gothic windows.

The chapel (and library above) was built by the master mason Bartholomew Peisley I in 1680–82, and with its giant order of attached columns and original cross-shaped stone-mullioned windows is architecturally the most ambitious building in the quadrangle. The timber screen, stalls and east end were all made in 1682 by Arthur Frogley, and survive intact. The 1865 glass in the east window is by Edward Burne-Jones, William Morris and Philip Webb.

The east end of the north range was built about 1746 to match the west end: only a vertical joint below the sundial separates the more than 150 years between the two. The dormer windows are modern. The President's lodging was extended into the south range in 1826, and the rest of this range was completed in 1927 by R Fielding Dodd.

ADDRESS Queen's Lane
ACCESS college open daily, daylight hours

Chapel: Bartholomew Peisley I (master mason) 1680–82 and others

Chapel: Bartholomew Peisley I (master mason) 1680–82 and others

St Edmund Hall, Kelly and Emden Buildings

This development, commissioned to provide new student rooms and a dining hall, occupies a centre-block site to the east of St Edmund Hall Front Quadrangle. The design consists of two parallel blocks running north–south, forming a new raised quadrangle, Upper Quadrangle, below which are service areas. The east range, set against the boundary, is single aspect and contains four storeys of student rooms. The west range, nearest Front Quadrangle, has a double-height dining hall on the ground floor with four storeys of student rooms above, and is dual aspect. There is a detached stair tower at the west end.

The architectural language is characteristic of the buildings of the period, a sort of refined brutalism. They are constructed of carefully controlled, board-marked concrete (as contrasted with Le Corbusier's *beton brut*), with blockwork infill panels and steel-framed glazing. The dining hall façade is divided into six bays. At the ground floor there are double-height columns, capped by segmental arches like those used by Basil Spence, the bays being infilled with large panes of glass. Above, horizontal bands of bay windows are slotted between heavy string courses which run at each floor level. At roof level a series of six triangular gables contains an attic level and produces the effect of a medieval skyline.

This little-known scheme should be noted for the ingenious way it slots such a vast building into such a small site.

ADDRESS Queen's Lane
ACCESS college open daily, daylight hours

Kenneth Stevens Associates 1968–70

Kenneth Stevens Associates 1968–70

St Edmund Hall, Library (formerly St Peter-in-the-East)

St Peter-in-the-East was sympathetically converted to a library for St Edmund Hall in 1970 by John Allen of Douglas Stevens Partners, having formerly been a parish church near the east gate of the medieval town.

Excavations have revealed signs of a Saxon church, but the earliest existing part is a Norman crypt of c.1120–30. This was originally accessed by two staircases leading down from the nave, with a small relic chamber between. Access now is from external staircases each side of the chancel, built into massive buttresses. The crypt is large, and has a stone vault supported by squat columns with scalloped capitals, some of which are carved.

The present church dates from c.1130 to 1140, and the north chapel was added c.1230–40, possibly by St Edmund of Abington. In the early 1300s the nave was extended westwards and the tower built. The north aisle was rebuilt in the mid-fourteenth century, and in the mid-to-late-fifteenth century the chancel and nave were heightened and rereofed, a two-storey porch added, and various windows replaced. The building is therefore a marvellous mixture of features covering nearly 400 years of building activity, among which the south door in the porch survives from the late twelfth century. Its chevron, beak-head and diaper ornament recall similar doorways at St Mary the Virgin, Iffley (page 80).

Today the tower is used as a bookstore, with a fellow's room above. The librarian's study is above the porch, there are bookstacks in the north aisle and the west part of the nave, and the nave and chancel have reading desks.

ADDRESS Queen's Lane, via St Edmund Hall
ACCESS college open daily, daylight hours; access to crypt only

Twelfth century, Douglas Stevens Partners 1970

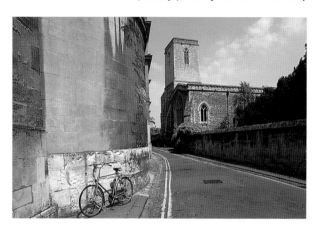

Twelfth century, Douglas Stevens Partners 1970

Wadham College, Main Quadrangle

Nicholas Wadham died in Somerset in 1609, and his wife, Dorothy, sent William Arnold, a local mason, to Oxford to build the new college founded by her husband's will.

The college took three years to build on old orchards north of the city walls. Arnold, who was renowned for good-quality work, constructed a quadrangle of three storeys following the example of John Akroyd at Merton College (page 296). He imposed a regular and symmetrical design on the entrance elevation and quadrangle, while fitting distinctive gabled attics between tall chimneys on the outer faces of the side ranges.

A fan-vaulted central gate tower, originally the Warden's lodging, directs the view axially to the frontispiece opposite. This has superimposed Classical Orders, like Merton, and separates the symmetrically placed (and indistinguishable) antechapel and hall, each with four windows of Jacobean strapwork tracery. The antechapel, on the left, is entered through a Renaissance classical doorway. The chapel projects to the east, and with the antechapel has a T-shaped plan in the New College tradition, and gothic window tracery. The right-hand matching doorway is blind, the stairs to the first floor hall rising instead through the frontispiece. The hall has a finely crafted hammerbeam roof, retains its central smoke lantern and, like the chapel, has an original oak strapwork screen.

Behind the hall, a library wing, with the kitchen on the ground floor, mirrors the projecting chapel, and the two enclose an east-facing, one-sided cloistered walk.

ADDRESS Parks Road
ACCESS college open daily: term 13.00–16.30; vacation 10.30–11.45, 13.00–16.30

William Arnold (master mason) 1610–13

William Arnold (master mason) 1610–13

Wadham College, Bowra Building

This design for new student residences on a tight site on the east side of the Junior Common Room Quadrangle is very ingenious. It places a linear podium containing communal facilities at ground-floor level, with a single aspect to the quadrangle, on top of which is a pedestrian street, accessed via external stairs from the north. The street has an intimate, almost medieval, scale and flavour, and is cleverly aligned so that the vista towards the south terminates on the bell tower of New College (page 236). Access to the student rooms, which are grouped off communal stairs in the traditional Oxford manner with four rooms per floor over three floors, is from this street. On the street's east side, forming the boundary to Manchester College, the houses are grouped into a continuous terrace. On the west side the houses are separated and read more like towers, allowing glimpses from the street into the landscaped quadrangle.

Each block of rooms is given the form of a four-square, brick tower with applied bay windows, topped by a double-height clerestory, which is in turn surmounted by a delicate floating flat roof. Stone is used for the dressings to the corners of the towers (for an appearance of strength), for the vertical mullions of the bays, and for the podium.

The building is carefully and deliberately designed and detailed using quality materials which have been carefully crafted. Even if the language could be thought of as slightly overworked, the building attempts to reinterpret the medieval scale of its surroundings, and as such makes a valuable contribution to the contemporary debate about contextualism.

ADDRESS Parks Road
ACCESS college open daily: term 13.00–16.30; vacation 10.30–11.45, 13.00–16.30

MacCormac Jamieson and Prichard 1992

MacCormac Jamieson and Prichard 1992

Wolfson College

If St Catherine's College (page 250) is classical in a neutral sense, Wolfson College, also of the 1960s, is classical in a committed, site-specific sense. If the first is Nordic in its restraint, this is Mediterranean in its full-bloodedness and is influenced by Le Corbusier.

Oxford's first graduate college required many accommodation types (houses, flats, study-bedrooms), and for its egalitarian social programme spaces for a shop, crèche and café beside the entrance, as well as a library, hall, buttery and seminar rooms. There was to be no chapel, the pyramidal roof over the hall instead providing a visual symbol of community. The magnificent rural site overlooks the river Cherwell, where a 'harbour' has been formed. It also adjoins suburban north Oxford, which suggested that the principal entrance should be at once welcoming and defensive.

The entrance leads to Main Quadrangle, a formal colonnaded rectangle containing the hall and library. From here covered walkways lead to the flats in Tree Quadrangle and the housing enclave beyond (with covered parking below), and to a curving block of study-bedrooms enclosing a lawn falling away towards the river. The walkways, with their white circular concrete columns and narrow glazing moduls, recall Le Corbusier's convent at La Tourette near Lyons, while the south-facing cellular rooms, with their balconies defined by slab and cross-wall, are reminiscent of his Unité d'habitation in Marseille. Wolfson was a major step in a significant sequence of college commissions for Powell and Moya, including the Cripps Building, St John's College, Cambridge (1963), the Picture Gallery and Blue Boar Quadrangle, Christ Church (pages 284 and 286) and Queens' College, Cambridge (1971).

ADDRESS Linton Road, east end
ACCESS apply to porter's lodge

Powell and Moya 1969–74

Powell and Moya 1969–74

Colleges: south of St Mary's

Campion Hall

When the mercurial Jesuit and apologist for English catholicism Father Martin D'Arcy, recently elected Master of Campion Hall, approached Sir Edwin Lutyens in 1933 to help him choose a site for the hall's new Oxford building, Lutyens was already an eminent architect at the height of his career. His work at New Delhi was complete, as were his designs for the unrealised Metropolitan Cathedral at Liverpool.

Lutyens designed a restrained L-shaped building of three storeys raised above a half basement, whose two wings enclose a private garden at the rear of the site. It is built entirely of coursed-rubble stonework, with unadorned recessed stone-mullioned windows. The block facing the street is austerely understated, with a simple arched doorway and a minimum of fenestration. The chapel on the top floor has distinctive arched windows, and uses the roof space for extra height internally. The garden wing houses the library and refectory on the ground floor, with rooms for 30 students on the two storeys above. Here the windows, staggered vertically, are larger, and broad steps lead up centrally from the lawn to a classical doorway.

Knowing this would be his only building in Oxford, Lutyens took a close interest in all the details, personally designing the oak furniture. His natural sense of humour found expression in the chapel lights, which are modelled on cardinals' birettas. The bells incorporated into the capitals at the garden entrance are a pun on 'Campion', and may also refer to his work at New Delhi.

ADDRESS Brewer Street
ACCESS by appointment; visible from Brewer Street

Sir Edwin Lutyens 1934–36

Sir Edwin Lutyens 1934–36

Christ Church Cathedral

St Frideswide priory was founded early in the twelfth century and was dissolved in 1524 by Cardinal Thomas Wolsey, who demolished the western part of the church and cloister for the new quadrangle of his Cardinal College. Henry VIII made it Christ Church chapel, and in 1546, despite its smallness, he made it a cathedral, a unique sharing by college and diocese. Of the priory buildings there remains a mid-thirteenth century chapter house and Norman doorway, a Perpendicular gothic cloister of c.1500, and the dormitory and refectory, now college rooms.

Today's church was built from 1194, and the late Norman chancel, transepts and nave are stylistically similar to the lower part of the tower. Unusually, the nave arcade has an attached giant order of two storeys. The attached columns have an entasis, and their capitals are almost Roman in style, while the arches are heavily undercut to emphasise their grandeur. The slightly later nave clerestory has pointed arches, a style further developed when the upper stage of the tower, with its pinnacles and spire, was built in the mid-thirteenth century.

The chancel clerestory was rebuilt shortly before 1500 to support a magnificent new vault. It is similar to that of 1480–83 in the Divinity School (page 98) and may also have been designed by William Orchard. Great arches with lantern pendants, in imitation of a timber hammerbeam roof, support square bays of intricate star-lierne vaulting. The transept ceilings are of about the same date. In 1870 Sir George Gilbert Scott restored the cathedral, rebuilding the east wall, and adding a bay and new entrance to Tom Quadrangle to the west.

ADDRESS St Aldate's; access from Broad Walk
ACCESS Monday–Saturday 09.30–18.00, Sunday 12.45–17.30
(October–12 April closes 16.30); admission charge

Late twelfth–fifteenth centuries

Late twelfth–fifteenth centuries

Christ Church, Tom Quadrangle and Hall

In 1524 Cardinal Thomas Wolsey dissolved St Frideswide's priory, creating a site for his new Cardinal College. He had built the south range of the quadrangle, including the hall and kitchen, and two-thirds of the east and west ranges, including the lower part of the great gate tower (page 274), before his fall from Henry VIII's favour halted work in 1529. His masons were John Lubbins and Henry Redman. Humphrey Coke built the magnificent timber hammerbeam roof in the first-floor hall. At that time the long frontage to St Aldate's was only two-thirds built, but the great tower at the south end, with its early Renaissance details, was complete. The great chapel proposed for the north side to rival that at King's College, Cambridge, the cloister around the quadrangle, and the free-standing bell tower – like that at Magdalen College (page 226) – were only at foundation level. Henry VIII refounded the college in 1532, calling it Christ Church. He decided to retain the church, making it both college chapel and cathedral (page 270), and probably appropriated the already prefabricated timber roof of Wolsey's chapel for use at Hampton Court.

In 1638–48 Dean Samuel Fell fan-vaulted the hall staircase (the present stairs were designed in 1805 by James Wyatt), and his son, Dean John Fell, completed the quadrangle in 1660–86, including the street frontage, gate tower, round fountain, and the wall arcades, raised terrace and buttresses, which recall Wolsey's earlier plan for a vaulted cloister.

The battlemented parapets, pinnacles on the hall, bell tower, stair turrets, and statues above the hall entrance, and the cathedral entrance are all by George Bodley and Thomas Garner, built in 1876–79.

ADDRESS St Aldate's; public access via cathedral
ACCESS college open Monday–Saturday 09.30–18.00, Sunday 12.45–17.30 (October–12 April closes 16.30); admission charge

John Lubbins and Henry Redman (master masons) 1525–29

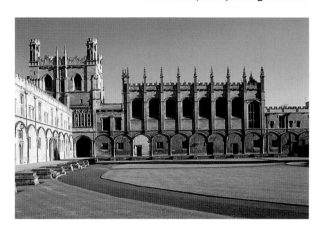

John Lubbins and Henry Redman (master masons) 1525–29

Christ Church, Tom Tower

Cardinal Thomas Wolsey's gateway was to be a suitably wide and magnificent entrance to the Great Quadrangle of his Cardinal College (page 272). Only the flanking turrets and arch, with its original door, were completed by him in 1525–26, and these use the architectural language of the finest late Perpendicular gothic style of the time. The lowest stage of the turrets consists of a sequence of angular bays formed in plan by superimposed squares. These are surmounted by octagonal piers, and all is covered with narrow blind panels, a language similar to that employed at the recently completed Henry VII's Chapel at Westminster Abbey.

A century and a half after Wolsey's fall from power, Sir Christopher Wren, in 1681, was asked by Dean John Fell to complete the great gate tower. Although not incorporating an observatory as Fell wanted, he none the less gave Christ Church one of Oxford's best-known monuments. Despite being a convinced classicist, Wren opted for the gothic style 'to agree with the founder's work', though not 'so busy'. As at his St Mary Aldermary in London, a contemporary gothic design, Wren used ogee domes to cap the turrets, and the same window types and roof form for the tower, producing his own grand, but simplified, version of the gothic style. He also designed the gothic fan-vault inside the arch.

The name of the tower refers to the sonorous medieval bell, Tom, which was moved from the cathedral, recast and hung in the tower in 1684.

ADDRESS St Aldate's
ACCESS none; visible from St Aldate's

J Lubbins and H Redman (master masons) 1525–26, C Wren 1681–82

J Lubbins and H Redman (master masons) 1525–26, C Wren 1681–

Christ Church, Peckwater Quadrangle

Henry Aldrich became Dean of Christ Church in 1689. Despite his many academic interests and reputation for conviviality, he also found time to be an authoritative architectural adviser and an architect in his own right. He was consulted on the design of Trinity College chapel, designed All Saints church (page 164), and probably designed the Fellows' Building at Corpus Christi (page 290). For his own college he designed Peckwater Quadrangle, to replace a quadrangle of medieval buildings. The mason was William Townesend.

The residential quadrangle has three identical sides of three storeys, in the classical style. Each has a rusticated base supporting a giant order of pilasters, with a central pediment supported on attached columns. Aldrich also designed a fourth side as a focus for the quadrangle. This was intended to be a free-standing range with full-height columns, surmounted by a cupola. In the event, this side was built as a library (page 278) after Aldrich's death in 1710, to a different design by Dr George Clarke, Aldrich's friend and architectural successor.

Aldrich's classical approach was an outright rejection of the backward-looking traditionalism of contemporary work at Oriel and University Colleges (pages 298 and 310), although its rigidity lacked the flair of the more full-blooded contemporary Oxford designs of his friend Nicholas Hawksmoor. Aldrich's limitations as a designer are apparent both in his simple juxtaposition of three identical blocks, and in his failure to place pilasters in the corners where the ranges meet.

ADDRESS access from Broad Walk, via cathedral
ACCESS college open Monday–Saturday 09.30–18.00, Sunday 12.45–17.30 (October–12 April closes 16.30); admission charge

Dean Henry Aldrich 1707–14

Dean Henry Aldrich 1707–14

Christ Church, Library

Dr George Clarke, a gifted amateur architect and fellow of All Souls College, was the friend and architectural successor of Dean Henry Aldrich, and after Aldrich's death in 1710 Clarke inherited his design for a free-standing residential building intended as a focus for Peckwater Quadrangle (page 276). The college decided it instead needed a library to house, among other bequests, Aldrich's own library. Clarke designed a new building, reducing the number of storeys, making the bays wider and fewer, removing the cupola, and proposing an open piazza below the library at ground level.

After trying out various elevational treatments, Clarke settled on one reminiscent of Michelangelo's Capitoline Palace in Rome, at once monumental and grave under its deep entablature, and baroque in spirit: a splendid contrast with the rest of Aldrich's more anodyne quadrangle. The central entrance leads under the building to the rear, where a double staircase, projecting at the back of the building, sweeps up to enter the superb first floor room centrally. The fine stucco ceiling, wall panels and fittings are by Thomas Roberts in the 1750s.

In 1764–72 the college enclosed and fitted out Clarke's piazza to house the collection of Old Master pictures given by General John Guise. After the building's 1962–64 refacing in contrasting white Portland and brown Clipsham stones, Clarke's magnificent library can now be appreciated in its original splendour.

ADDRESS access from Broad Walk, via cathedral
ACCESS college open Monday–Saturday 09.30–18.00, Sunday 12.45–17.30 (October–12 April closes 16.30); admission charge

Dr George Clarke 1717–38

Dr George Clarke 1717–38

Christ Church, Canterbury Quadrangle

When Christ Church acquired the adjacent run-down Canterbury College, they employed James Wyatt to redevelop the site. Wyatt was 27 years old and had studied architecture in Italy. He was familiar with the work of the Adam brothers, Robert and James, and had already achieved renown through his Pantheon in Oxford Street, London, completed in 1772. Later, during a prolific career, he was also to build in Oxford the Radcliffe Observatory (page 152) and a new library at Oriel College (page 300).

Wyatt produced a refined classical design for the new three-sided Canterbury Quadrangle, which is elegant and understated, and relates skilfully to the adjacent buildings. From outside the college, the entrance (from the south-west corner of Oriel Square) is through a screen wall which incorporates a fine Adamesque triumphal arch. This is placed on axis with the end wall of Dr George Clarke's magnificent library of 1717–38 (page 278). This, with its grand Venetian window, becomes the focal point of the quadrangle towards which the gravelled surface gently rises.

On the inside, the central arched gateway is surmounted by a pediment, and the inward-looking quadrangle is of two storeys. The north range is terminated by the three-storey return wall of Peckwater Quadrangle (page 276), with its rusticated base and tall pilasters, designed by Dean Henry Aldrich in 1707–14. Opposite this Wyatt placed a matching end pavilion to complete the symmetry of his quadrangle, while using the same window proportions elsewhere for continuity.

ADDRESS Access from Broad Walk, via cathedral; exterior visible from Oriel Square
ACCESS college open Monday–Saturday 09.30–18.00, Sunday 12.45–17.30 (October–12 April closes 16.30); admission charge

James Wyatt 1773–83

James Wyatt 1773–83

Christ Church, Meadow Buildings

Long vilified as a 'Victorian monstrosity', Meadow Buildings is typical of new High Victorian gothic college residential buildings brought about by the growth of the university in the second half of the nineteenth century.

Sir Thomas N Deane's partner Benjamin Woodward had died of consumption in 1861, shortly after the completion of their University Museum (page 118), leaving Deane to continue the Dublin practice. Woodward's love of John Ruskin's Venetian gothic lives on here, with Venetian balconies and doors on the south elevation, and the bands of coloured stone that give the building a striated appearance when it is not covered in summer by Virginia creeper. Elsewhere the windows are simple lancets.

Raised on a half basement, the building is three storeys high with a fourth attic floor. Its great length is divided into bays by slender full-height arched windows that light the stairs, and the building is enlivened by a roofscape of dormer windows and chimneys. A great tower marks the central route through the building.

The setting is magnificent. The building sits alongside the Broad Walk, a formal but spacious tree-lined promenade laid out in the late seventeenth century. Beyond is Christ Church Meadow, an ancient area of grazing bounded by the rivers Isis and Cherwell. During the 1960s and 1970s there were repeated attempts to build a relief road across these meadows, but it was not to be – common sense finally prevailed.

ADDRESS Broad Walk, off St Aldate's
ACCESS none; visible from Broad Walk and from the north when the cathedral is open

Sir Thomas N Deane 1862–66

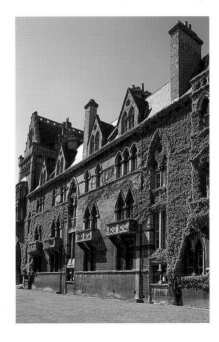

Sir Thomas N Deane 1862–66

Christ Church, Picture Gallery

In the early 1960s Powell and Moya were commissioned by Christ Church to design a new public art gallery for the large collection of Old Masters and Italian Primitives previously kept below the library. The site given was part of the Deanery Garden and was already enclosed by buildings or high stone walls. The gallery entrance was to be through the south range of Canterbury Quadrangle. The challenging brief insisted on minimum impact, and Powell and Moya's ingenious design was indeed tantamount to being invisible.

Their solution was to design a single-storey, L-shaped building buried 1.5 metres below ground level, thus keeping the height below the existing stone walls. The gallery turns away from the Deanery, and the L-shaped plan forms a small courtyard around which the circulation is disposed. The only views to the outside are into this courtyard, thus producing an intimate, internalised space. The small galleries are entered directly from the glazed circulation route, and are carefully lit by concealed skylights. A delightful sequence of spaces opens from the narrow entrance through Canterbury Quadrangle, past the reception into the glazed linear circulation with galleries off, and ends in the darkened drawings gallery.

The architectural language is consistent with the architects' other Oxbridge college work, such as St John's College Cripps Building (1963–66), Cambridge. The plan and section have great clarity, the detailing is refined and minimal, and the materials – Portland stone, bronze, concrete, rubble stone, plaster – are exploited for their natural qualities. The building is a fine, if modest, essay in 1960s British modernism.

ADDRESS from Broad Walk, via cathedral
ACCESS open Monday–Saturday 10.30–13.00, 14.00–17.30, Sunday 14.00–17.30 (October–March closes 16.30); admission charge

Powell and Moya 1964–67

Powell and Moya 1964–67

Christ Church, Blue Boar Quadrangle

Following the success of Powell and Moya's design for its Picture Gallery (page 284), Christ Church commissioned the same architects to design new student residences on a tight linear site behind the high stone wall that forms the college's northern boundary to Blue Boar Street. The building runs parallel with the wall, and returns at each end help define a new quadrangle, Blue Boar Quadrangle.

The elevation is divided into bays by a series of expressed stone-clad cross walls, which alter their geometrical alignment to take up the irregularities of the site boundary. The vertical circulation occupies a separate link bay every six bays. Each bay contains one student room on each floor level. The rooms have a single aspect looking into the quadrangle. On the quadrangle side the repeated stone piers, which project boldly from the main façade, create a strong imagery. The infill panels are of full-width glazing alternating with precast concrete spandrel units. A clerestory-like penthouse contains lecturer's sets, which are roofed in lead and give a modulated roof line.

The elevation to Blue Boar Street is different and more interesting. The building is designed to read as a series of linked towers which project rather austerely above the existing high stone wall. Each tower is individually expressed by recessing the links. Portland stone walls form strong corners to the towers, which are punctuated by vertical strips of glazing, or applied square projecting bays, reinforcing their monumental, fortress-like appearance. The picturesque irregularity of the alignment of the towers gives the façade an interesting syncopated rhythm along its length.

ADDRESS St Aldate's
ACCESS none; partly visible from Blue Boar Street

Powell and Moya 1968

Powell and Moya 1968

Corpus Christi College, Front Quadrangle

Five decaying academic halls between Merton College and St Frideswide's priory were demolished to create the site for Corpus Christi College. Front Quadrangle, the first part of the college, was built within four years, from 1512. Its intimate scale enhanced by the memorable central sundial of 1581 is charming.

The three-storey gate tower originally housed the President's lodging, which was reached by the adjoining stair tower. The hall, conveniently nearby, is in the north-east corner of the quadrangle, and originally presented a gable to the street. The fine hammerbeam roof is by Humphrey Coke, who became Henry VIII's master carpenter in 1519, and later built the hall roof in Christ Church (page 272). The wall panelling is of 1700. Behind is the kitchen, which was part of one of the academic halls that predated the quadrangle.

The chapel adjoins the south-east corner of the quadrangle and extends the south range, which also houses the library, furnished in 1604. The chapel was built with a cloister on its south side, which was later redeveloped to form the cloister for the Fellows' Building (page 290). The extension of the chapel into the south range took place in 1675-76, giving an antechapel, and a fine classical carved cedarwood screen was added.

Originally the quadrangle had two storeys, to which an embattled parapet was added in 1624, but removed internally in 1935. Externally, a third storey was added to the Merton Street and west-facing frontages in 1737 to add height to earlier attics. The frontispiece facing the gate was added only in 1817.

ADDRESS Merton Street
ACCESS college open daily 13.30–16.30

William Vertue and William Est (master masons) 1512–16

William Vertue and William Est (master masons) 1512–16

Corpus Christi College, Fellows' Building

In 1706 the sixteenth-century cloister to the south of Corpus Christi College chapel was cleared away to make room for a new residential building and cloister, given by Thomas Turner, President of the college from 1687 to 1714.

Formerly known as Turner's Building, the main building is a free-standing three-storey block, for which a precedent had been set in 1665 by Sir Christopher Wren at Trinity College (page 188). The architect is unknown, but was probably Dean Henry Aldrich, whose Peckwater Quadrangle at Christ Church (page 276) has a similar Palladian style. William Townesend was master mason, and it is possible that he designed the building himself, with Aldrich's help.

The south front contains the main rooms, looking out over Merton Field beyond the line of the city walls, which enclose the adjacent fellows' garden. The three central bays are given emphasis by Ionic pilasters and a pediment. At each end of the building a bay projecting at the rear gives the end elevations added depth, that to the west having alcoves and blind windows facing a garden. The projecting bays adjoin a three-sided classical cloister, or arched colonnade, built as part of the scheme in the space between the Fellows' Building and the chapel, to replace that demolished. The cloister, the smallest in Oxford, was originally of one storey, but more recently had another added above the east and west ends.

ADDRESS Merton Street, south side
ACCESS college open daily 13.30–16.30

Dean Henry Aldrich (attributed) 1706–12

Dean Henry Aldrich (attributed) 1706–12

Merton College, Chapel

Walter de Merton intended a fine chapel for the college he founded, of which the present one is only a part. Sadly, the idea of nave and aisles was abandoned in 1515 when that part of the site was conveyed to Corpus Christi College. Nonetheless, the T-shaped plan of choir, crossing and transepts (or antechapel) influenced later chapels such as those at All Souls, Magdalen and New College (pages 204, 224 and 234).

The exceptionally long choir (1290–97) and its refined window tracery and buttresses are typical of the late thirteenth century. The east window of seven lights and a rose is particularly fine, and all the side windows have the original stained glass. A sacristy was added to the south side of the choir in 1309–11, about the time that Mob Quadrangle (page 294) was started. The tower crossing was built in 1330–35; the south transept about 35 years later. In 1416–25 the north transept was built, and the windows of the south transept were changed to match, creating a very grand antechapel. The chapel was finally re-dedicated in 1425.

In 1448–51 the tower was built by master mason Robert Janyns Sr, who also worked at All Souls (1438–43). His tower has eight pinnacles, a pierced battlemented balustrade, and three square buttresses on each side with very large openings between – it is a stately piece of work.

The choir screen has recently been reassembled from the remains of one designed by Sir Christopher Wren, which was removed by William Butterfield when rebuilding the chancel roof in 1849–50. The gallery around the crossing was added in 1843–44 for bell ringing. The Tournai double plate lectern is early sixteenth century and is particularly rare.

ADDRESS Merton Street
ACCESS college open Monday–Friday 14.00–16.00, Saturday–Sunday 10.00–16.00

1290–1425, Robert Janyns (master mason) 1448–51

Colleges: south of St Mary's

1290–1425, Robert Janyns (master mason) 1448–51

Merton College, Mob Quadrangle

Mob Quadrangle is the oldest quadrangle in Oxford. It was built piece-meal and was not designed as a unified composition, but it soon estab-lished a precedent for other college quadrangles.

The two-storey east range, built first in 1308–09, includes a first-floor college treasury roofed in stone for security. This range abuts the chapel sacristy of 1309–11, to which it gives access. The north range probably dates from 1335 to 1336, and is thought to occupy the site of the old parish church of St John, acquired by Walter de Merton to allow him to build his new chapel (page 292). The south and west ranges were built in 1371–78 as an L-shaped, two-storey block with a library on the first floor, and they complete the quadrangle. The arrangement of narrow windows between the bookstalls was evidently inadequate, as in 1623 handsome dormer windows were added to let in more light. The library ceiling is early sixteenth century, and the fittings early seventeenth century, arranged by Sir Henry Savile, Fellow of the college and joint founder of the Bodleian Library (page 102).

ADDRESS Merton Street
ACCESS college open Monday–Friday 14.00–16.00, Saturday–Sunday 10.00–16.00

1304–07, 1371–78

1304–07, 1371–78

Merton College, Fellows' Quadrangle

Fellows' Quadrangle is entered through the gatehouse erected in 1497–1503 by Warden Fitzjames. This gateway and the adjacent two-storey bay window of the same period were built on the end of the hall, and together they form the north range, on to which Fellows' Quadrangle was added in 1610. The late thirteenth-century hall, remodelled and largely rebuilt by James Wyatt in 1790–94, and again by Sir George Gilbert Scott in 1872–74, forms a fine backdrop to the quadrangle.

Expansion of the college started in 1606 with the addition of a kitchen to the south of the hall, followed in 1608 with foundations for the rest of the quadrangle. The warden, Sir Henry Savile, employed John Akroyd, a fellow Yorkshireman, as master mason, and the whole scheme was built with great speed between March and September 1610. The design is straightforward, with simple regularly spaced arch-headed windows, and is notable as the first three-storey quadrangle in Oxford. A four-storey frontispiece of superimposed classical orders, intermixed with gothic details, faces the entrance. The gothicising battlemented parapet was added 12 years later.

The outside of the quadrangle is less restrained, with gables, tall chimneys, and two oriel windows facing the line of the city wall to the south, against which maintenance access (now the college garden) had to be left. The gate to the garden through the frontispiece was made in 1625–26, and in 1680 the senior combination room was made above the kitchens.

Savile and Akroyd were to collaborate soon after on the Bodleian Library Schools Quadrangle (page 102).

ADDRESS Merton Street
ACCESS Monday–Friday 14.00–16.00, Saturday–Sunday 10.00–16.00

John Akroyd (master mason) 1610

John Akroyd (master mason) 1610

Oriel College, Front Quadrangle and Middle Quadrangle

Oriel's medieval buildings were redeveloped piecemeal to a unified plan when the college was totally rebuilt under Provost John Tolson in the early seventeenth century. The west and south ranges of Front Quadrangle are of 1620–22; the north and east ranges are of 1637–42.

The residential ranges are of three storeys, with attractive, double-curved gables somewhat reminiscent of medieval attics. The gate tower, with its finely carved original doors, battlemented parapet, stair turret and stone fan-vault, also feels distinctly medieval.

The east range, facing the entrance, contains the hall on the first floor to the left. The hall is entered via the central porch and has a fine hammer-beam roof. The buttery and antechapel are on the right, with the chapel projecting behind, angled to suit the adjacent street. The contrived symmetry of the façade recalls Wadham and University Colleges (pages 260 and 310). Six identical windows with Jacobean gothic tracery, matching those in the chapel, are flanked by two Perpendicular gothic oriel windows, a pun on the college's name. Above the porch, with its parapet of Jacobean openwork lettering and strapwork, are three gothic alcoves with statues, and a classical segmental pediment. The pediment is rather French in style and is of the same stylistic family as the door-heads around the quadrangle. This mix of styles is typical of the age.

To the north, Middle Quadrangle has two buildings in an almost identical style, but built in 1720 and 1729 by William Townesend. The open quadrangle's conservative design provides a parallel with Radcliffe Quadrangle at University College (page 312), also built by Townesend.

ADDRESS Oriel Square
ACCESS college open daily 14.00–17.00

1620–42, William Townesend 1720, 1729

Colleges: south of St Mary's

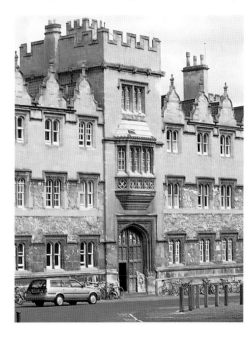

1620–42, William Townesend 1720, 1729

Oriel College, Library

In 1786 Oriel College received a bequest from Lord Leigh that doubled the size of its library. Finally abandoning its previous ultra-conservative approach to architecture (page 298), the college commissioned James Wyatt to design a new library in the classical style as an end stop to Back Quadrangle. Wyatt had made his Oxford debut with Canterbury Quadrangle at Christ Church (page 280), finished just five years previously.

The refined two-storey library is seven bays wide and has a giant order of attached Ionic columns standing on a rusticated arcaded base, an elegant development of a pavilion-library type already explored in 1692 by Dean Henry Aldrich at Queen's College (page 244) and in 1716 by Dr George Clarke at Christ Church (page 278). In Oriel's case, however, the arcaded ground floor was designed to be enclosed and to provide common rooms for the fellows – the first such purpose-built accommodation in Oxford. The main staircase is at the left-hand end of the building, the door on the right leading to the common rooms.

The first-floor library is furnished entirely with wall bookcases, some accessed by a slender gallery, which leaves the central space uncluttered. At one end there is an apse screened in the Adamesque manner by two giant columns, while at the other end Wyatt lined an adjoining room with late seventeenth-century panelling removed from New College Chapel, where he was working at the time (page 234).

ADDRESS Oriel Square
ACCESS none; college open daily 14.00–17.00

James Wyatt 1788–92

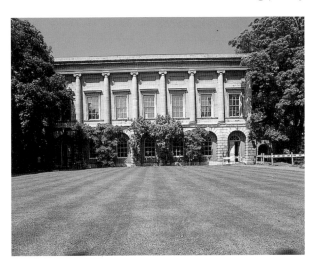

James Wyatt 1788–92

Pembroke College, Chapel and Garden Quadrangle

After its foundation in 1624 on the site of Broadgates Hall, Pembroke College continued an agreement to use the south aisle of St Aldate's church as its chapel, instead of building a new chapel as part of its development. This proved to be an inadequate arrangement, and in 1728 a new chapel was started on one side of the Commoners' Garden, abutting the west range of the Main Quadrangle. The design of the chapel is attributed to William Townesend, an important Oxford master mason and architect who built a number of college buildings (pages 246 and 298). The chapel is severely classical, unrelieved by tower or cupola. The garden front is entirely rusticated above the plinth, and a central emphasis is given by four Ionic pilasters. The doorway, with its mannerist pediment, fights the otherwise restrained symmetry of the façade, while a tall parapet imparts a feeling of forcefulness.

Inside, the fine screen and stalls are contemporary, but the Renaissance feeling of the rest of the interior dates from the 'restoration' in 1883–85 by Charles E Kempe, who installed stained glass, a new ceiling, and a marble altar.

The magnificent hall in the Perpendicular gothic style at the end of Garden Quadrangle, and the four-storey north range which faces the chapel, were designed and built by John Hayward in 1844–48 on the remains of the formal seventeenth-century gardens.

ADDRESS Pembroke Square
ACCESS apply to porter's lodge

William Townesend (attributed) 1728–32, John Hayward 1844–48

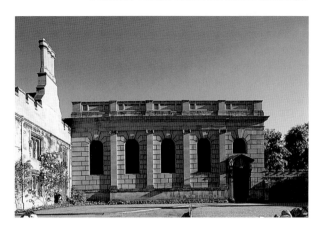

William Townesend (attributed) 1728–32, John Hayward 1844–48

Pembroke College, Sir Geoffrey Arthur Building

Maguire and Murray were the winners of an open competition held in 1986 for the design of a new residential building for Pembroke College, on a river side site near Folly Bridge (page 42).

The design takes its cue from the Oxford quadrangle and wraps the accommodation around two linked courtyards. The collegiate, inward-looking, form seems particularly appropriate, producing a feeling of community, and providing security and shelter for the exposed site. The arrangement of the accommodation also repeats the collegiate tradition of private rooms accessed off communal staircases. In this case there are six rooms to each stair, with a communal kitchen and bathroom at the top. The common rooms are located around the entrance, adjacent to the porter's lodge.

Both the layout and architectural language are relaxed and pictur-esque. The courtyards are shaped to the site rather than imposing a strict formal geometry. In addition, the building massing is designed to look informal, with fragmented pitched roofs, projecting bays and dormers, and the relaxed placement of punched window openings. The skilful use and detailing of the materials – untreated oak for the windows, Spanish slate for the roofs, and banded fairfaced concrete blockwork (in imitation of stone) for the walls – all contribute to the comfortable, if architecturally undemanding, medieval ambience of the building.

ADDRESS Marlborough Road
ACCESS none; visible from river walk

Maguire and Murray 1989

Colleges: south of St Mary's

Maguire and Murray 1989

St Hilda's College, Garden Building

University expansion during the late 1960s led to a plethora of architectural commissions from colleges to provide additional student accommodation. The all-women's St Hilda's College engaged Alison and Peter Smithson, leading architects of the British new-brutalist movement of the 1950s, to design a new residential building with 48 study-bedrooms.

The building was designed as a four-storey pavilion on one side of an informal garden quadrangle at the southern end of the college. Despite the different context, the design bears certain formal similarities to the Smithsons' earlier Economist Headquarters at St James's Street, London (1960–64), primarily in the pavilion form, the wrapping of rooms (residential in place of offices) around a service core, and in the layering of the façade. Indeed, it is the design of the façade which gives the Garden Building its great charm and delicacy.

The Smithsons employ a post-and-beam language on the exterior which seems to evoke both primitive and classical origins. The posts are of precast concrete and are part of the load-bearing frame structure, but the timber lattice beams, whose functional role is to provide screening for the rooms and support for the vegetation that overruns the building, are non-load-bearing. With this composition the Smithsons came close to their declared aim of achieving 'the gentlest of styles'.

ADDRESS Cowley Place
ACCESS college open daily: term 14.00–17.00; vacation closed

Alison and Peter Smithson 1970

Alison and Peter Smithson 1970

St Hilda's College, Jacqueline du Pré Building

This modest auditorium was commissioned as a memorial to Jacqueline du Pré, the cellist and member of St Hilda's College who died at a young age from multiple sclerosis. The new building sits alongside the dull neo-Georgian Wolfsen Building designed by Albert Richardson and Simon Houfe in 1963, and extends the length of the south range of the quadrangle known as St Hilda's South.

The auditorium is presented as a 'blank box' of buff-coloured brickwork, with a hipped slate-covered roof behind a parapet. The box is divided along its length into five-fielded bays, capped by a modest decorative brick cornice at parapet level. The entrance is marked by a two-storey glazed slot with small punched square windows on each side. Internally the building has a more complex plan than might be expected from the exterior. The doorway leads into a delightful octagonal timber-lined foyer, with a gallery at first-floor level. This space has a pyramidal ceiling, and is lit by a lantern at the apex. It gives access to ancillary accommodation at ground- and first-floor levels. A small lobby leads to the main space, the auditorium, which is a simple rectangle with a rather heavily detailed first-floor balcony.

The auditorium is reputed to have good acoustics, partly as a result of the *in-situ* concrete roof, and the design is a bold response to the architectural programme, the building's context, and the limited budget.

ADDRESS Cowley Place
ACCESS college open daily: term 14.00–17.00; vacation closed

Van Heyningen and Haward 1995

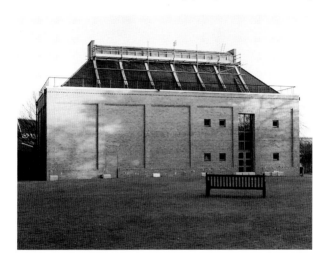

Van Heyningen and Haward 1995

University College, Front Quadrangle

In 1634 two benefactions allowed University College to redevelop its medieval site by building a new, unified quadrangle.

The effectiveness of small gables *en masse* had already been shown at Oriel College (page 298). Richard Maude started the three-storey west range by placing the chimneys on the outside, using string courses to order the windows, and crowning the walls with the same ogee gables he had already used at St John's College Canterbury Quadrangle (page 174). The north range was similar, and incorporated a traditional gate tower with a gothic fan-vault in the gateway.

In 1637 Maude started the chapel and hall that form the south range, using the well-tried end-to-end plan first used at New College (page 234); using the symmetry, Jacobean gothic tracery and Renaissance frontispiece of Wadham College (page 260); and crowning the design with more ogee gables. Chapel and hall doors were placed side by side in the centre, while the hall on the right was, unusually, at ground level with the kitchen behind. Work was abandoned during the Civil War, and the east range was not completed until 1677.

Henry Keene remodelled the hall in 1766 in the gothic revival style, using a plaster fan-vaulted ceiling, which was removed in 1904 to reveal the original timber roof. In 1802 the hall and chapel range was made more genuinely 'gothic' by replacing the gables with pinnacles (now removed), lengthening the window tracery, and remodelling the frontispiece. In the chapel the glass, screen, stalls and reredos are all seventeenth century, but in 1862 Sir George Gilbert Scott remodelled the interior in a thirteenth-century style, while rebuilding the east end and raising the roof.

ADDRESS High Street, south side
ACCESS apply to domestic bursar

1634–77, Richard Maude (master mason) 1634–42

1634–77, Richard Maude (master mason) 1634–42

University College, Radcliffe Quadrangle

Dr John Radcliffe, the renowned physician, left money in his will for the founding of a new hospital, a new building for the Bodleian Library (page 112), and a new quadrangle at University College. His will instructed that the design 'be answerable to the old': no doubt he had happy memories of his undergraduate days in the college.

The east range of Front Quadrangle had been completed in 1677, and its rear elevation became the west elevation of Radcliffe Quadrangle when work on it began 39 years later. The college took Radcliffe at his word, and the architecture was identical, complete with the by-now outmoded small ogee gables. The college's frontage to High Street was doubled in length, and a second, almost identical, gate tower built. This even had a traditionally constructed gothic fan-vault, the last of its kind to be built in the country.

The existing east range of Front Quadrangle dictated the alignment of the plan of Radcliffe Quadrangle, which was open to a garden on its south side. Because the two new ranges also follow the line of perimeter streets they were, unusually, both made wedge-shaped in plan so that the quadrangle could be square. This is most noticeable at the south end of the east range, which becomes so shallow that it does not need windows on Logic Lane.

ADDRESS High Street
ACCESS apply to domestic bursar

William Townesend 1716–19

William Townesend 1716–19

Index

Oxford: an architectural guide

Oxford: an architectural guide

also available from ellipsis

london: a guide to recent architecture
Samantha Hardingham
A snapshot of London, with a wave of Lottery-funded projects and the
Jubilee Line Extension designed by the UK's most exciting architects, while
the Millennium Dome provides a controversial full stop to the century.
ISBN 1 899858 92 X

eat london: architecture and eating
Samantha Hardingham
An updated edition of the best-selling guide to London's flourishing
restaurant scene. This book describes a key factor in the success or failure
or any restaurant – its design.
ISBN 1 84166 003 5

gay london: a guide
William McLoughlin *et al*
Much more than a mere listing, this guide provides an insight into how
a gay man might enjoy the more esoteric pleasures the city has to offer,
from the pursuit of spectral figures in Abney Park Cemetery to contem-
plation of exactly what form the muse took that inspired Frederic Lord
Leighton when building his house in Holland Park.
ISBN 1 899858 73 3

art london: a guide
Martin Coomer
From the artist-run or alternative spaces of the East End to the blue-chip
showrooms of the West End, and beyond, this is a vibrant and opinion-
ated tour of spaces for contemporary art, encompassing the key person-
alities and most exciting exhibitions of the last few years.
ISBN 1 899858 75 X

PRICE £8.00

Samantha Hardingham

London

A guide to recent architecture

· · ·

samantha hardingham

eat london

architecture eating and drinking

· · ·

jones, mcloughlin, martin, wyllie

gay london

a guide

· · ·

martin coomer

art london

a guide to contemporary art spaces

· · ·

· · ·

bath: an architectural guide

The city of Bath sits in a bowl of hills at the southern tip of the Cotswolds, at a point where the River Avon forms a loop around a short peninsula. It was here that the Romans established their city of Aquae Sulis, and it was here too that eighteenth-century society settled in the refined luxury of the architecture we now call Georgian. This is the architecture that gives this comparatively small city its international reputation.

The built scenery is dramatic. When viewed from one of the hilltop vantage points, the light-golden local stone seems to be everywhere, relieved only by the green roofs of the Snowhill Housing Estate on the east side and the blue gas holders to the west.

But Bath is not just a museum of a long-passed social phenomenon. It is a living urban organism, of just about the right size to live in. The Victorians and Edwardians built here, sometimes indecorously, and contemporary architects including Nicholas Grimshaw, Aaron Evans and the Brutalist Smithsons have work worth visiting in or near the city. This guide covers all of Bath's notable architecture, with specially commissioned photographs, and an introduction outlining the social and economic forces that have shaped the city.

ISBN 1 899858 28 8
PRICE £8.00

Thom Gorst